FREEDOM
THAT LASTS ®

GROWING AND CHANGING GOD'S WAY

JIM BERG

Freedom That Lasts is a
ministry of

Faith
BAPTIST CHURCH

Freedom That Lasts® - **Level 2: Growing and Changing God's Way**
Jim Berg

All Scripture is quoted from the Authorized King James Version unless otherwise noted.

Design and page layout by Sarah Forsythe and Peter Crane

Freedom That Lasts® is a registered trademark of Faith Baptist Church, 500 West Lee Road, Taylors, SC, 29687

www.freedomthatlasts.com.

© 2014 by Faith Baptist Church, Taylors, South Carolina 29687
Printed in the United States of America
All rights reserved
ISBN 978-0-9853333-1-7
V.1

TABLE OF CONTENTS

INTRODUCTION

Congratulations!

You have reached an important milestone!

Having finished the first student manual in *Freedom That Lasts,* you have . . .

- memorized 83 verses and character definitions,
- written eight reports,
- read dozens of chapters in Proverbs,
- attended many church services, and
- served the Lord through several service opportunities.

The day you finished the book was, no doubt, a big day in your life! You can enjoy wearing your Bronze Freedom Pin on your nametag, but most of all you can experience a much greater freedom from the power of sin in your life as you "continue in the things you have learned" (2 Timothy 3:14).

Your first student manual helped you take a look at the *target* of biblical change—the character of Jesus. It taught you what a disciple of Jesus Christ should look like according to the virtues of 2 Peter 1.

The second and third manuals will focus more specifically on the *process* of how that change towards Christlikeness takes place.

This second level will involve Scripture memory, service projects, church attendance, and so forth like the first student manual. It will, however, contain a great deal more reading. The reading segments (usually the first five checkpoints) contain much valuable information to help you understand the process of changing and growing to be more like Jesus Christ.

Part of some memorization checkpoints will be re-memorizing key verses from the first student manual when those verses have special applications to the new material you are learning about in this manual.

Let's think about biblical change for a moment.

Do We Know What We Are Doing?

Has anyone ever told you that you need to change something—your attitudes, your desires, or your actions—and inside you agreed that things needed changing, but you didn't have a clue about how to get started?

Christopher Columbus set out to discover a westward passage to Asia and didn't know how to get there either. He ended up in an entirely different place—North America! Some unknown writer has proposed the following award in his memory for those who imitate him.

Christopher Columbus Award

This award goes to those who, like good old Chris, when they set out to do something, don't know where they are going; neither do they know how to get there. When they arrive, they don't know where they are, and when they return, they don't know where they've been.

We can't blame our explorer friend for getting lost—he had a good idea, but no map. God, however, has given us a "map" telling us how to make lasting, godly change in our lives. In these studies, we will examine God's map for changing our lives to become more and more like Jesus.

God gives us a map for our sanctification—our changing to become more like Jesus Christ in our attitudes, desires, and actions. It is not a process that takes place all at once—as if someone "zapped" you on the head with a magic wand. It is *progressive*—that means it takes place little by little over a period of time. In the Bible it is called "growth."

If you understand this process, you will know how to address problems in your life—now and in the future—and you will know how to help others with their problems. So, let's get started in our study as we discover how we can be *Growing and Changing God's Way.*

UNIT 1

CHANGE

> I beseech you therefore, brethren, by the mercies of God, that ye present your bodies a living sacrifice, holy, acceptable unto God, which is your reasonable service. And be not conformed to this world: but be ye transformed by the renewing of your mind, that ye may prove what is that good, and acceptable, and perfect will of God.
> (Romans 12:1-2)

CHECKPOINT 1 – NOT JUST ANY CHANGE WILL DO

You know by now that the subject we are discussing together is *change*, but for the Christian, not just any change will do. Look at the following situations that describe a change someone made—a change that was only outward.

Buddy stopped his pouting (a desirable change), but only because his parents gave in and bought him the car he wanted.

Julie stopped her constant complaining to her coworkers about her boss (a desirable change), but only because her boss transferred to another store.

As you can see, we have to be more specific about what kind of change we are talking about and how it is accomplished. A mere change in Buddy's or Julie's attitude does not necessarily mean that the *real* problem has been recognized and resolved. If you knew Buddy, you would know that his real problems are the selfishness and covetousness of his heart.

Lessons from a Tea Bag

Our problems come not from around us but from within us. We can illustrate this truth by thinking about a tea bag. When we place a tea bag into a teacup, and fill the cup with hot water, the water activates the tea in the bag, releasing its taste into the water around it.

1. Do the flavor and aroma of the tea come from the hot water or from the tea bag?

   _____

This is exactly what happens in your heart. The pressures and temptations around you merely *draw out* of your heart what is already in it. What is in your heart determines what comes out of your heart—anger, bitterness, despair, fear, deception, cruelty, or else, joy, kindness, helpfulness, and so forth—just as the contents of the tea bag determine the flavor and aroma that come out in hot water.[1]

2. Read Acts 16:16-25. Paul and Silas were put into a "hot water" situation. What came out of their "tea bag" in prison?

   _____

   _____

3. **Memorize Mark 7:21-23 (Memory Card 1).**

   For from within, out of the heart of men, proceed evil thoughts, adulteries, fornications, murders, thefts, covetousness, deceit, [sensuality, envy, slander], pride, foolishness: All these evil things come from within, and defile the man.

---

[1] Tea bag illustration adapted from J. Allan Peterson, *Your Reactions Are Showing* (Lincoln, Nebr.: Back to the Bible, 1967), 14-15.

8

4. **Rememorize 2 Corinthians 5:17 (Memory Card 2).**

> *Therefore if any man be in Christ, he is a new creature: old things are passed away; behold, all things are become new.*

To complete this checkpoint, you must read all the text, fill in the blanks, memorize Mark 7:21-23, and rememorize 2 Corinthians 5:17.

☐ Text read.............................Date completed: _____ Initials: _____

☐ Blanks filled in ....Date completed: _____ Initials: _____

☐ Mark 7:21-23 ....Date completed: _____ Initials: _____

☐ 2 Corinthians 5:17....................Date completed: _____ Initials: _____

I have completed Checkpoint 1.

_____   _____
Your name   Date

_____   _____
Group Leader's name   Date

CHECKPOINT 2 – THE GOAL AND PERSON OF CHANGE

The Goal of Change

Imagine watching a World Cup soccer game between the American and Brazilian teams for which no one had bothered to set up the goals at the ends of the field. The teams could scramble to take possession of the ball from each other, but then what would they do? They would have no goal to shoot at. There would be no way to keep score and no way to judge their progress.

Many Christians run around the field of their Christian life with just as much confusion because they do not know what the goal of the Christian life is. But God has given us a clear goal to aim for—the likeness of His Son, Jesus Christ. *Christ is the example of what a man can look like when that man is controlled entirely by the Holy Spirit and is in perfect fellowship with God.* The result is that a believer looks increasingly like Christ—the "grown-up Christian."

1. Write out Matthew 12:18 below.

   _____

   _____

   _____

   _____

2. What characteristic of Jesus Christ pleased the Father according to the verse above?

   _____

3. Read Philippians 2:5-11.

   ☐ Check this box when you have read the passage.

   Now check the answer below that best describes why God honored His Son, according to this passage.

   ☐ Jesus healed people while He was on the earth.

   ☐ Jesus was a humble servant who obeyed His Father's commands, even when it meant death.

   ☐ Jesus never mistreated anyone, even when He was being mistreated by others.

When a believer looks like a humble servant of the Father, he looks like Jesus Christ. But we need help for this kind of change.

The Person of Change

I grew up on my grandfather's large cattle farm in South Dakota. My favorite piece of machinery was a yellow bulldozer, a D6 Caterpillar. My grandfather used the "Cat" for moving small buildings and haystacks, digging a water reservoir, and pulling heavy equipment in the field.

Suppose my grandfather tried to pull by hand his several thousand pound disc-plow. What would happen? About all he would be able to do in his own power would be to lift the hitch off the ground. On the other hand, if he were first to start the "Cat's" powerful diesel engine and then hitch up the plow to it, he could get out into the field. Without the bulldozer, he would be helpless to get any serious plowing done.

In the same fashion, *the Holy Spirit is the divine power behind every change we need to make in the Christian life.* Without Him, change towards Christlikeness is impossible.

Who Is the Holy Spirit?

The Holy Spirit is not some mystical or cosmic impersonal influence or force. He is one of the three *Persons* of the Godhead—God the Father, God the Son, and God the Holy Spirit. He is the Agent who shows us our need for Christ and imparts Christ's life to us at salvation. He then begins the work of changing our lives to become like Christ through sanctification.

Ephesians 5:18 tells us to "be filled with [controlled by] the Spirit." The Holy Spirit lives within every believer, and through His convicting voice He attempts to *lead* us away from sin (see Romans 8:14). If we obey His convicting voice, we become more like Christ. We will begin to show the "fruit [results] of the Spirit"—the results of His work in our lives.

4. Read Galatians 5:22-23 and list below the evidence—"the fruit of the Spirit"—that will appear in the life of a believer who is obeying—being controlled by—the Holy Spirit.

_____

_____

_____

_____

5. If you have not been allowing the Holy Spirit to control you and produce His fruit, what is coming out of your "tea bag" instead of the fruit of the Spirit when you are in "hot water" situations?

    _____

    _____

    _____

    _____

6. **Memorize Galatians 5:22-23 (Memory Card 3).**

    But the fruit of the Spirit is love, joy, peace, longsuffering, gentleness, goodness, faith, meekness, temperance . . .

7. **Memorize Galatians 5:16 (Memory Card 4).**

    This I say then, Walk in the Spirit, and ye shall not fulfil the lust of the flesh.

To complete this checkpoint, you must read all the text, fill in the blanks and memorize Galatians 5:22-23 and Galatians 5:16.

☐ Text read.................................Date completed: _____ Initials: _____

☐ Blanks filled in ....Date completed: _____ Initials: _____

☐ Galatians 5:22-23.......................Date completed: _____ Initials: _____

☐ Galatians 5:16 ....Date completed: _____ Initials: _____

I have completed Checkpoint 2.

_____   _____
Your name   Date

_____   _____
Group Leader's name   Date

CHECKPOINT 3 – THE PROCESS OF CHANGE

Someone has said that sanctification is the "Christianizing of the Christian." Unfortunately, all of us are aware of Christians who do not seem to be very Christian. Yet God has a definite plan whereby we can become like Christ.

1. Look up the verses in the following chart and fill in the blanks.

    Please note that the blank spaces correspond to the KJV Bible. If you are not using a KJV Bible, fill in the blanks with the corresponding words for the translation you are using. You will use this same tactic for any future blanks you need to fill in.

Our Personal Responsibility	Paul's Instruction (Ephesians 4:22-24)	The Holy Spirit's Result
1. Mortify the flesh	22) "That ye _____ _____ concerning the former conversation [your previous lifestyle] the [ways of] the old man [the old unsaved self], which is _____ according to the deceitful _____";	The flesh is *restrained* through the Holy Spirit's help.
2. Meditate upon the Word	23) "And be _____ in the spirit of your _____";	The mind is *renewed* through the Holy Spirit's illumination.
3. Manifest Christlikeness	24) "And that ye _____ _____ [the ways of] the new man [the new self in Christ], which after God is created in _____ and true _____."	Christ is *reflected* to others through the Holy Spirit's fruit.

Caution: While every believer has a personal responsibility to carry out these commands, the Bible clearly teaches that these activities can be performed *only* with the help of the Holy Spirit. Keep in mind that sanctification has been designed by God to be a *cooperative venture between God and us.* He works in us but expects us to work at change too.

2. Memorize this definition of sanctification (Memory Card 5).

> *Sanctification is that process whereby the Spirit of God uses the Word of God to make us like the Son of God amidst the circumstances we face in the providence of God.*

The various parts of the definition above should become clearer as you go through this study.

Understanding Discipleship

While this student manual is about *sanctification*—God's plan for helping us change and grow—it is also about *discipleship.* Biblical discipleship is not primarily a program. It is a certain kind of relationship between two believers with a very specific goal in mind.

3. Memorize this definition of discipleship (Memory Card 6).

> *Discipleship is helping another believer make biblical change toward Christlikeness.*

4. Before you read the definition above, what did you think discipleship was? If you haven't thought about it before, write that in the blank.

_____

_____

Since discipleship is helping another believer make biblical change toward Christlikeness, it ought to be a *primary concern* in several relationships of life: friend to friend, coach to athlete, Christian teacher to student, Christian employer to employee, pastor to congregation, and so forth.

None of these relationships will fulfil God's goal for change unless the people involved understand *sanctification* and *discipleship.*

To complete this checkpoint, you must read all the text, fill in the blanks, and memorize the definitions for sanctification and for discipleship.

☐ Text read...Date completed: _____ Initials:_____

☐ Blanks filled in ....Date completed: _____ Initials:_____

☐ Definition of Sanctification....Date completed: _____ Initials:_____

☐ Definition of Discipleship.......Date completed: _____ Initials:_____

I have completed Checkpoint 3.

_____	_____
Your name	Date
_____	_____
Group Leader's name	Date

CHECKPOINT 4 – MORE ABOUT DISCIPLESHIP

It is important for you to pay attention to what God is doing in you through this study so that He can call on you to help others as well. Please don't look at these checkpoints merely as an assignment that you hurry up and finish so that you can get it over with and get on to something else. Unless you have a long-range perspective as you study, you will soon forget much of what you learn. You will need this information—sooner than you think!

1. **Memorize 1 Timothy 4:15-16 (Memory Card 7).**

   Meditate upon these things; give thyself wholly to them: that thy profiting may appear to all. Take heed unto thyself, and unto the doctrine; continue in them: for in doing this thou shalt both [help] thyself, and them that hear thee.

God has placed others around you who need to grow in Christ. All believers are to take up the challenge to "admonish one another" (Romans 15:14) and to "exhort one another" (Hebrews 3:13).

The writer of Hebrews warned that those who "ought to be teachers," based upon the length of time they have been saved, but who are not actively teaching others, should place themselves under some basic instruction again. He charged them with being "dull of hearing" and "unskilful in the word of righteousness" (Hebrews 5:11-14).

This passage in Hebrews 5 contradicts those who say, "Religion is a personal matter; I don't meddle in other people's lives" or "It's his life; if he wants to throw it away, that's his business." The apostle insists that those who don't want to "interfere" in the lives of others need biblical change themselves. They are being self-centered by refusing to help others who need it.

2. **Read Luke 10:25-37.**

    ☐ Check this box when you are finished.

3. Who are the people in your life that need help?

    _____

    _____

4. Are you more like the Good Samaritan in this passage, who was willing to get involved, or are you like the Levite and the priest who hurriedly walked by so that they wouldn't have to do anything?

    _____

In some situations you should *not* try to do the discipling yourself—a woman shouldn't be the primary spiritual help for a man; a person who is spiritually weak himself shouldn't be helping someone who will pull him down; a son or a daughter isn't the primary one to help a parent with a spiritual problem. *In cases such as these a spiritually mature adult should be the primary rescuer. Your responsibility would be to get your friend or relative to someone who can help.* You certainly wouldn't try to perform an operation on a friend who is bleeding internally because of a car accident. You would do your part to get him to someone who knows what he is doing and can do it safely.

The thought of helping others may be quite scary right now, but by the end of these units, you should have a good idea of how to help others. You must start with "meditat[ing] upon these things" and "giv[ing your]self wholly to them" first, as we have seen. Stay with us. There is much more ground to cover!

To complete this checkpoint, you must read all the text, fill in the blanks, and memorize 1 Timothy 4:15-16.

☐ Text read.............................Date completed: _____ Initials: _____

☐ Blanks filled in ....Date completed: _____ Initials: _____

☐ 1 Timothy 4:15-16 ....Date completed: _____ Initials: _____

I have completed Checkpoint 4.

_____   _____
Your name   Date

_____   _____
Group Leader's name   Date

CHECKPOINT 5 – JOURNAL WORK

To complete this checkpoint you must journal five days in a row.

I have completed Checkpoint 5.

_____   _____
Your name   Date

_____   _____
Group Leader's name   Date

CHECKPOINT 6 – CHURCH ATTENDANCE

To complete this checkpoint, you must do the following:

1. Attend two or more church services within one week. They can be the Sunday morning worship service, a Sunday school class, a Sunday evening service, or a midweek service (sometimes called "prayer meeting").

2. Fill in the information below, and have a pastor of the church sign the proper blank below.

   Name of the church: _____

   Check the services you attended:

   ☐ Sunday school

   ☐ Sunday morning worship service

   ☐ Sunday evening service

   ☐ Midweek service

   ☐ Other (explain): _____

   Pastor's signature: _____

I have completed Checkpoint 6.

Your name _____   Date _____

Group Leader's name _____   Date _____

CHECKPOINT 7 – WRITTEN REPORT ON "CHANGE"

To complete this checkpoint, write a one-page paper explaining the important truths you have learned in this lesson. To write the paper you will need to review your answers to remind yourself of what you have learned. Grammar and spelling are not an issue. Do the best you can, asking God to help you understand the importance of learning the process of how we grow and change.

I have completed Checkpoint 7.

_____   _____

Your name   Date

_____   _____

Group Leader's name   Date

CHECKPOINT 8 — SERVICE OPPORTUNITY

An important part of Christian living is serving God and others. One way of serving is to tell others how they can find the help you are getting. To complete this service project, pass out fifteen pieces of literature—either fifteen flyers for *Freedom That Lasts* or fifteen gospel tracts. You must personally hand each piece of literature to a person and invite him to read it. You may not merely leave them somewhere for people to pick up on their own.

You might say something such as "Hey, do you know anyone who is struggling with an addiction? Would you give this to them? They can get help at this class."

Remember that God promises to supply everything you need to do His will—even the grace (the divine help) to do something as challenging as passing out Christian literature. This exercise will give you a good opportunity to put into practice what you have learned in this chapter about trusting God for what you need.

Write out below where you distributed these pieces of literature.

_____

_____

_____

_____

_____

I have completed Checkpoint 8.

_____   _____
Your name   Date

_____   _____
Group Leader's name   Date

CONGRATULATIONS!

You have completed the eight checkpoints necessary to finish your study on "Change." The road map towards growth and change into Christlikeness should be clearer to you now.

When you finish all the checkpoints for this unit and your group leader has signed off on them, you will receive your reward at the end of that class. We encourage you to invite your friends and family to witness your accomplishment.

If you will continue the lessons in this book and faithfully use your *Spiritual Life Journal*, you will come to know your God much, much better than you do now!

UNIT 2

THE FLESH

> There is a way which seemeth right unto a man, but
> the end thereof are the ways of death.
> (Proverbs 14:12)

CHECKPOINT 1 – GETTING THE VIEW OF MAN RIGHT

In the last unit we took a glimpse of the "big picture" of biblical change. It is like the picture on the front of a puzzle box. Part of the "big picture" is the right view of man. To have the wrong picture on the front of the puzzle box is as frustrating as having no picture at all. In this unit we will see the true picture of man as God gives it to us in His Word, and we will find out what happens when people have the wrong picture.

The Real Culprit

When Adam and Eve listened to the Devil in the Garden of Eden, an evil nature was placed within man. The Bible calls it the "flesh". *The flesh feeds into the mind of man a continual flow of information that is set against God.* Before a person is saved, he *must* obey that sinful part of his nature. It is always telling him to please himself, protect himself, assert himself, love himself, indulge himself—basically, to serve himself.

Although the absolute power of the "old man"[2] over us is broken at salvation, we still possess a leftover effect of that "old man." We still have an indwelling principle of sin—the flesh—that corrupts every part of us. *It is in constant conflict with the Spirit of God and tempts us to make life work apart from God.* It is the source of our tendency to dethrone God and to view ourselves as the one who should rule our lives.

1. Look up the following verses and list some of the characteristics of the flesh—that "indwelling principle of sin" mentioned in these verses and in the paragraphs above. Here are the verses: Romans 7:15-25, Romans 8:6, and Galatians 5:17.

   _____

   _____

   _____

   _____

   _____

No honest man can deny that something is desperately wrong with mankind. Unfortunately, we often do not understand the treachery that lies in our heart. We sometimes think we are pretty good people who "mess up" once in a while. The biblical picture—the true picture of man on the puzzle box—is just the opposite: we are all pretty bad people who do right only by the grace or help of God.

As we look at our flesh—our sinful nature, you may be sickened by what you see, but stay with the study. We must see what is wrong with man. *Remember that though you may be saved, you still have within you all the potential for evil that any unsaved person has.* The

---

[2] The "old man" is the Bible's term that describes all we are as a result of Adam's fall (Romans 5:12) and is our state before we are saved.

difference is that you do not have to live for yourself as your flesh dictates, but your unsaved friend does.

2. Read Romans 3:10-18 and list below the characteristics of the human heart that Paul outlines in that passage. Remember that these tendencies are present in every person—even after salvation.

_____

_____

_____

_____

_____

_____

_____

3. Memorize 1 Corinthians 15:22 (Memory Card 8).

For as in Adam all die, even so in Christ shall all be made alive.

To complete this checkpoint, you must read all the text, fill in the blanks, and memorize 1 Corinthians 15:22.

☐ Text read.......................................Date completed: _____   Initials: _____

☐ Blanks filled in ....Date completed: _____   Initials: _____

☐ 1 Corinthians 15:22..................Date completed: _____   Initials: _____

I have completed Checkpoint 1.

Your name	Date
Group Leader's name	Date

CHECKPOINT 2 – HAVE IT YOUR WAY

Years ago a popular fast-food chain advertised its hamburgers by telling customers that they could have any number of options on their burgers. They wanted you to come in and "have it your way." That appealed to the most basic desire of man's sinful nature. *Man left to himself wants his own way.*

1. Isaiah exposes the very essence of this rebellion in Isaiah 53:6. Look it up and write out the verse below.

_____

_____

_____

_____

Our biggest problem then is not the environment in which we have been reared; it is not the evil that has been done to us by others; it is not the limitations we feel so acutely. Our biggest problem is a heart that wants its *own way* in opposition to God's way.

2. Look up the passages below, fill in the blanks, and consider how often God targets man's own way as his most basic problem.

    *   "Every man did that which was right in his
        _____ _____" (Judges 17:6).

    *   "So I gave them up unto their _____
        _____ _____: and they walked in their _____ _____" (Psalm 81:12).

    *   "Trust in the Lord with all thine heart; and lean not unto thine _____ _____"
        (Proverbs 3:5).

- "Be not wise in thine _____
  _____; fear the Lord, and depart from
  evil" (Proverbs 3:7).

- "The way of a fool is right in his _____
  _____" (Proverbs 12:15).

- "Cease from thine _____
  _____" (Proverbs 23:4).

- "He that trusteth in his _____
  _____ is a fool" (Proverbs 28:26).

- "Woe unto them that are wise in their _____
  _____, and prudent in their
  _____ _____" (Isaiah
  5:21).

- "Be not wise in your _____
  _____" (Romans 12:16).

- "[Love] doth not behave itself unseemly [not rude], seeketh
  not her _____" (1 Corinthians 13:5).

- "For all seek their _____, not the
  things which are Jesus Christ's" (Philippians 2:21).

- "For men shall be lovers of their _____
  _____" (2 Timothy 3:2).

- "These are murmurers, complainers, walking
  after their _____
  _____" (Jude 16).

This *own way* tendency of our flesh is the culprit. The apostle Paul
testified in Romans 7:21, "I find then a law [a consistent principle
of life] that, when I would do good, evil is present with me." Three
verses earlier (v. 18) he said, "For I know that in me (that is, in my
flesh), dwelleth no good thing: for to will [to do right] is present
with me; but how to perform that which is good I find not." This is
what we are up against. Our natural response to all this ugliness is
to cry out with the apostle Paul, "O wretched man that I am! Who

shall deliver me from the body of this death?" (v. 24). Fortunately, Paul didn't stop there. This blessed apostle who knew full well by experience and by revelation the treachery of his own heart followed that cry of desperation with a glorious statement of triumphant hope.

3. Write out Romans 7:25—his statement of triumphant hope.

_____

_____

_____

_____

_____

There is a way out! There is deliverance! There is hope! And with that the apostle Paul launches into the instruction of how to "walk after the Spirit" in Romans 8.

But before we can get to that discussion of Romans 8, we need to get a more detailed picture of our sinful nature. We want a full picture, not just a passing glimpse. We don't want the biblical view of our heart to be soon forgotten. We will be taking some close-up looks at the ugly nature of the indwelling sin principle in the next couple of checkpoints.

4. **Memorize Romans 7:25 (Memory Card 9).**

    I thank God through Jesus Christ our Lord. So then with the mind I myself serve the law of God; but with the flesh the law of sin.

To complete this checkpoint, you must read all the text, fill in the blanks, and memorize Romans 7:25.

☐ Text read.........................Date completed: _____ Initials: _____

☐ Blanks filled in ....Date completed: _____ Initials: _____

☐ Romans 7:25 ....Date completed: _____ Initials: _____

I have completed Checkpoint 2.

Your name _____ Date _____

Group Leader's name _____ Date _____

CHECKPOINT 3 – THE FLESH DEFIES GOD

Often we do not discover the true force of our sinful nature against God until we begin to serve God wholeheartedly.

This is very much like the experience of one who is rowing a canoe. As long as he is going *with* the current, he has no idea how strong the current really is. Only when he decides to turn his canoe around and start rowing *against* the current does he experience its true strength.

If you are always giving in to the pull of your sinful heart, you never learn the extent of its power over you. If you decide to "row upstream," however, you will meet full force the "current" of indwelling sin. You will quickly realize that going against the sinful bent of your heart is not only difficult—it is impossible on your own. You will learn how desperately you need God.

1. Read Isaiah 55:6-9 and fill in the blanks below.

   "Seek ye the Lord while he may be found, call ye upon him while he is near: let the wicked forsake _____ _____, and the unrighteous man _____ _____: and let him return unto the Lord, and he will have mercy upon him; and to our God, for he will abundantly pardon. For _____ _____ are not _____ _____, neither are _____ _____ _____ _____, saith the Lord. For as the heavens are higher than the

earth, so are _____ _____
higher than _____ _____,
and _____ _____
than _____
_____."

There can be no doubt that God sees our independent spirit—the very thing the world considers a virtue—as the root problem of man. Our heart says, "I will make life work *my own way!*" Here then is the defiance of our flesh. Paul says it is "enmity [deep-seated defiance] against God: for it is not subject to the law of God, neither indeed can be" (Romans 8:7).

This fleshly nature is constantly at war with God. It is no wonder, then, that when we begin to obey God's Word with the help of God's Spirit, our flesh rises up and resists that work of God.

2. Read Matthew 26:41 and 1 Corinthians 10:12 and summarize below the nature of the warnings to you contained in these verses.

_____

_____

_____

_____

No wonder the wisest man, Solomon, said, "He that trusteth in his own heart is a fool" (Proverbs 28:26). A traitor lives within us! It cannot be trusted. It cannot be pacified. And until we reach heaven, it cannot be removed.

3. **Memorize Matthew 26:41 (Memory Card 10).**

    Watch and pray, that ye enter not into temptation: the spirit, indeed, is willing, but the flesh is weak.

4. **Memorize 1 Corinthians 10:12-13 (Memory Card 11).**

    Wherefore let him that thinketh he standeth take heed lest he fall. There hath no temptation taken you but such as is common to man: but God is faithful, who will not suffer you to be tempted above that ye are able; but will with the temptation provide a way to escape, that ye may be able to bear it.

To complete this checkpoint, you must read all the text, fill in the blanks, and memorize Matthew 26:41 and 1 Corinthians 10:12-13.

- ☐ Text read.............................Date completed: _____ Initials: _____

- ☐ Blanks filled in ....Date completed: _____ Initials: _____

- ☐ Matthew 26:41 ....Date completed: _____ Initials: _____

- ☐ 1 Corinthians 10:12-13...........Date completed: _____ Initials: _____

I have completed Checkpoint 3.

_____   _____
Your name   Date

_____   _____
Group Leader's name   Date

CHECKPOINT 4 – THE FLESH DEFILES MAN

Although some people will acknowledge the essential wickedness within man, they fail to understand the penetrating nature of its influence. In some ways the effects of the sinful nature on every part of man are like smoke damage in a house fire. Even if only one part of the house is destroyed before the fire is extinguished, the smoke penetrates every other part of the house as well. It seeps into the closets, gets inside boxes of clothes in the attic, and smells up every article of clothing in the dresser drawers. Nothing escapes its penetration.

The Bible teaches that sin has infected every part of man's being. We call this truth "total depravity." Man is depraved—fundamentally crooked. Total depravity does not mean that an individual man is as wicked as is possible but that his fundamental crookedness has penetrated his total being. No part of his body or of his heart is left untouched.

Survey the Damage

- The sin principle has darkened man's *understanding* (Ephesians 4:18; 1 Corinthians 2:14) so that without God's help he cannot understand spiritual things.

- Our *will* has been made stubborn by the influence of indwelling sin. The "blindness of their heart" in Ephesians 4:18 can be translated "hardness" or "stubbornness."

- Our *mind* and its *affections* have been perverted so that we need continual reminders to "set [our] affection [mind] on things above, not on things on the earth" and "seek those things which are above" (Colossians 3:1-2).

- Our *conscience*—that part of us that tells us we are doing something wrong—is dulled so it is not as quick to sound an alarm when we are indulging in sin. In some people it is entirely deadened so that they no longer feel anything negative about sin (Ephesians 4:19).

In short, there is not a single part of the soul—the inner man— that has not been injured by indwelling sin. We must face the fact that we are thoroughly contaminated by indwelling sin.

This is why God so forcefully warns us about the dangers of living "after the flesh"—following after its pull.

1. Look up the following verses and fill in the missing words to see God's warnings about giving in to the sinful nature within.

    - "For if ye live after the _____, ye shall _____ [be destroyed]: but if ye through the Spirit do mortify [a term we will discuss later] the deeds of the body, ye shall _____ " (Romans 8:13).

- "Abstain from _____
_____, which _____
against the soul" (1 Peter 2:11).

- "This I say then, Walk in the Spirit, and ye shall
not fulfill the _____ of the
_____. For the flesh lusteth [sets its
desires] against the Spirit, and the Spirit against the flesh: and
these are _____ the one to
the other so that ye cannot do the things that ye would [if
you give in to the flesh]" (Galatians 5:16-17).

- "For he that _____ to his
_____shall of the flesh reap _____"
(Galatians 6:8).

There is hope for us, but it certainly will not be found by
looking within ourselves. Our only hope is for some "outside"
intervention. We must not become confident within ourselves
or trust ourselves. Even though the absolute power of this sinful
bent is broken at salvation, the internal corruption still remains
while we are on this earth. It is always present and active. We
must not forget about it or fail to arm ourselves against it.

2. **Rememorize Galatians 6:7-9 (Memory Card 12).**

   *Be not deceived; God is not mocked: for whatsoever a man soweth,
   that shall he also reap. For he that soweth to his flesh shall of the
   flesh reap corruption: but he that soweth to the Spirit shall of the
   Spirit reap life everlasting. And let us not be weary in well doing:
   for in due season we shall reap, if we faint not.*

To complete this checkpoint, you must read all the text, fill in the
blanks, and rememorize Galatians 6:7-9.

☐ Text read.........................Date completed: _____   Initials: _____

☐ Blanks filled in ....Date completed: _____   Initials: _____

☐ Galatians 6:7-9................Date completed: _____   Initials: _____

I have completed Checkpoint 4.

_____   _____
Your name   Date

_____   _____
Group Leader's name   Date

CHECKPOINT 5 – THE FLESH DECEIVES AND DESTROYS MAN

Perhaps you are saying right now, "Do we have to look at this picture in any more detail? Can't we just leave things here and go on?" We could if God had not wanted us to know more. But He has wisely chosen to show us two other aspects of man's sinful tendency that we must consider before moving on to other topics.

The first is the deceptive nature of man's heart. We all know by experience the intrinsic pull to be dishonest. None of us had to be taught to lie. Lying came naturally to us the first time we did it, and it continues to be natural.

1. Look up the following verses and fill in the missing words to see God's perspective about the deceitfulness of our heart.

   • "But exhort one another daily . . . lest any of you be hardened through the _____ of sin" (Hebrews 3:13).

   • "The heart is _____ above all things, and desperately wicked" (Jeremiah 17:9).

   • "But be ye doers of the word, and not hearers only, _____ your own selves" (James 1:22).

As you learned in the first student manual, "behind every fall is belief in a lie." Not only does the world lie to us, but we also lie to _ourselves_, and we believe the lies of others. The lies are about ourselves, lies

32

about God, and lies about how to live on this fallen planet. Believing lies will always destroy us.

The Worst Thing That Could Happen

The Bible teaching is plain and simple, "And sin, when it is finished, bringeth forth *death* (James 1:15); "For if ye live after the flesh, ye shall *die*" (Romans 8:13). Death means separation from something. Of course, the death spoken of in these verses cannot mean eternal separation from God, for these passages are written to believers. Satan's design is to separate the believer from his Master's fellowship, rendering him useless in the Master's service.

Our flesh is so destructive that rather than demanding our *own way*, we ought to be begging God never to let us have what our flesh demands. We ought to pray, "Dear God, limit me, bind me, restrict me. Do whatever you have to, but please do not let me have my *own way*."

2. Be honest with yourself.

- When are you likely to be stubborn with God and demand your own way?

  _____

  _____

  _____

- How does your heart most often deceive you?

  _____

  _____

  _____

- In what areas of your life do you see sin's destruction already making headway?

_____

_____

_____

Can you see now why "doing right" is so hard? Can you also see why it is just not possible to live the Christian life on your own without God's help? You and I are no match for the evil that is within us. Do you see now why we don't have to look for any causes outside man himself to explain his behavior? A biblical look at the human heart is all the explanation we need to explain school shootings, drive-by shootings, domestic violence, serial killings, and so forth. People committing these crimes have not "snapped" or "gone off the deep end." They are showing the effects of "grown-up sin" in the heart.

The picture is bleak. If there were no help from God, knowledge of this condition would lead only to despair in the heart of any honest, thinking person. It ought to lead us rather to repentance for sin and trust in God for help. In the next unit we will begin to look at how we can effectively battle the inner war we experience.

3. Memorize Jeremiah 17:9 (Memory Card 13).

> _The heart is deceitful above all things, and desperately wicked: who can know it?_

To complete this checkpoint, you must read the text, fill in the blanks, and memorize Jeremiah 17:9.

☐ Text read...........................Date completed: _____ Initials: _____

☐ Blanks filled in ....Date completed: _____ Initials: _____

☐ Jeremiah 17:9 ....Date completed: _____ Initials: _____

I have completed Checkpoint 5.

_____   _____
Your name   Date

_____   _____
Group Leader's name   Date

CHECKPOINT 6 – JOURNAL WORK

To complete this checkpoint you must journal seven days in a row.

I have completed Checkpoint 6.

_____   _____
Your name   Date

_____   _____
Group Leader's name   Date

CHECKPOINT 7 – CHURCH ATTENDANCE

To complete this checkpoint, you must do the following:

1. Attend two or more church services within one week. They can be the Sunday morning worship service, a Sunday school class, a Sunday evening service, or a midweek service (sometimes called "prayer meeting").

2. Fill in the information below, and have a pastor of the church sign the proper blank below.

Name of the church: _____

Check the services you attended:

☐ Sunday school

- ☐ Sunday morning worship service

- ☐ Sunday evening service

- ☐ Midweek service

- ☐ Other (explain): _____

Pastor's signature: _____

I have completed Checkpoint 7.

Your name	Date
Group Leader's name	Date

CHECKPOINT 8 – WRITTEN REPORT ON "THE FLESH"

To complete this checkpoint, write a one-page paper explaining the important truths you have learned in this lesson. To write the paper you will need to review your answers to remind yourself of what you have learned. Grammar and spelling are not an issue. Do the best you can, asking God to help you understand the importance of learning the process of how we grow and change.

I have completed Checkpoint 8.

Your name	Date
Group Leader's name	Date

CHECKPOINT 9 — SERVICE OPPORTUNITY

An important part of Christian living is serving God and others. To complete this checkpoint, you must do one of the two following tasks:

1. Personally bring two people to attend a *Freedom That Lasts* class

   OR

2. Make two visits with your care group leader, FTL director, or other mature member of your church to follow up on visitors who have attended FTL or other church visitation prospects.

In the following blanks write the names of the people you brought to FTL or the names of the people you visited with your care group leader, and so forth.

While you are working on this checkpoint, you may start working on the next lesson. You won't be able to be signed off on any future checkpoints until this one is completed, so do your best to bring two people to class or to make two follow-up visits with an FTL or church leader.

_____

_____

I have completed Checkpoint 9.

_____	_____
Your name	Date
_____	_____
Group Leader's name	Date

CONGRATULATIONS!

You have completed the nine checkpoints necessary to finish this unit. The road map towards growth and change into Christlikeness should be clearer to you now.

When you finish all the checkpoints for this unit and your group leader has signed off on them, you will receive your reward at the end of that class. We encourage you to invite your friends and family to witness your accomplishment.

If you will continue the lessons in this book and faithfully use your *Spiritual Life Journal,* you will come to know your God much, much better than you do now!

UNIT 3

HUMILITY

> Know ye that the Lord he is God: it is he that hath made us, and not we ourselves; we are his people, and the sheep of his pasture.
> Psalm 100:3

CHECKPOINT 1 – DEPENDENT BY DESIGN

Trusting in our *own way* defies the most basic fact of our creation: *God made man dependent.* Man can no more joyfully and peacefully live independently from God than he can fly by flapping his hands. He was not made a bird. He was made without wings—by design. He was not made a self-contained, self-sufficient creature. He was made dependent—by design.

Man can make a space shuttle, build a house, manufacture a car, and construct a superhighway; but since none of these items are self-created, none of them are self-sustaining. They are dependent upon the one who made them. The space shuttle and the car have to be refueled and serviced. The house and the highway have to be repaired. Creation inherently demands dependency. Man can acknowledge this about everything he makes for himself in this world but rebels against the thought that somehow he is dependent upon his own Creator.

The governing principle here is that *if you needed someone to make you, you need someone to maintain you.* You must face your dependence, repent of any proud attempt to make life work your *own way*, and submit to the ways of your Creator. Perhaps a parable can show you how easy it is for us to think we are making life work on our own.

A Boy and a Bike

Six-year-old Johnny approaches his father with a request. The conversation goes something like this.

"Dad, I'm six now. Can I buy a bike?"

"Well, Son, I'm sure you are old enough to learn to ride, but how are you going to buy a bike?"

"I have a quarter, Dad! Remember, you give me a quarter every week when I help you wash the car. This week I saved it because I want to buy a bike. I didn't buy candy with it this week."

"You really are serious about buying a bike if you passed up candy. Well, if you think you are ready for a bike, go get your quarter and let's go shopping."

After checking out several stores, they find a bike that Johnny really likes. Johnny's father looks at the price tag and calculates that with tax the bike will cost one hundred dollars—a far cry from a quarter.

"Son, are you sure this is the bike you want?"

"I sure am! I've always dreamed about having a bike like this. This is the one I want—and I've got my quarter."

"OK, then; wheel the bike up to the counter, Johnny, and let's pay the clerk."

Johnny pushes the bike up to the checkout counter, lays his quarter on the counter, and says to the clerk, "I want to buy this bike." The clerk smiles at him, winks at his father, and replies, "Sure, Son, you've made a great choice." Dad turns to Johnny and says, "Son, take the bike outside and wait for me on the sidewalk. I want to talk to the lady." As Johnny leaves the store, his father writes out a check for

$99.75 and then joins his son outside. They load the bike into the car, and on the way home Johnny's father commends him for his choice.

> "Son, I just want to tell you how proud I am of you today. Every other week you have spent your quarter on candy and gum— things that would not last. This week you saved your quarter and decided to buy something that would be around for a while. That's a good decision, Son. I can tell you are growing up."

When they arrive home, they unload the bike, and Johnny runs into the house to get his mother. When she comes outside, Johnny exclaims, "Look at my new bike, Mom! Isn't it beautiful! And I bought it with my own money!"

1. Did Johnny's quarter really buy the bike?

   _____

2. Johnny contributed twenty-five cents. Who gave that to him?

   _____

3. So, who really bought the bike?

   _____

Someday Johnny will gain a better understanding of how life works and will learn that he didn't buy the bike. His quarter was a mere vote in the process saying that he wanted a bike rather than candy. His quarter, however, didn't buy the bike—he was dependent upon his father and didn't even know it. One day, if he remembers his words, he will be embarrassed by his ignorance.

4. What other things would a good father be providing for Johnny that Johnny may not even have stopped to think about?

   _____

   _____

   _____

5. Ready Daniel 4:28-37 to see a real-life account of an important man who thought "his quarter bought his bike.

☐ Check the box when you have read the passage.

6. Who was *really* responsible for all the king's successes?

_____

7. **Memorize James 1:17 (Memory Card 14).**

Every good gift and every perfect gift is from above, and cometh down from the Father of lights, with whom is no variableness, neither shadow of turning.

This verse teaches that God is the Giver of everything good we receive, and He never changes. He will always be a giver of good things. The words "no variableness, neither shadow of turning" mean that He does not change.

To complete this checkpoint, you must read all the text, fill in the blanks, and rememorize James 1:17.

☐ Text read......................................Date completed: _____ Initials: _____

☐ Blanks filled in ....Date completed: _____ Initials: _____

☐ James 1:17 ....Date completed: _____ Initials: _____

I have completed Checkpoint 1.

Your name _____   Date _____

Group Leader's name _____   Date _____

CHECKPOINT 2 – HUMILITY: THE SIGN THAT SHOWS YOU REALLY UNDERSTAND LIFE

"Humility is simply [man's] acknowledging the truth of his position as man and yielding to God His place."[3] Man's natural, fallen

---

[3] Andrew Murray, *Humility* (Springdale, Pa.: Whitaker House, 1982), 12.

tendency is to insist that he be left alone to live life his *own way* and to take credit for any successes and accomplishments he may experience along the way.

If we are to truly understand life, we must have a bigger picture of life than Johnny had in the parable about his bike. He thought that *he* bought the bike. He thought that *he* was the key factor in how life worked for him. He was unaware that everything he enjoyed in life was the result of someone else's resources, kindness, and help. We can excuse Johnny's limited view of life because he is but a six-year-old child. Sadly, however, even most adults—like Nebuchadnezzar, the king we saw in the last checkpoint from the book of Daniel— also think that they are the key factor in how life is working out for themselves.

Our pride shows itself in our lives in two ways. First, it manifests itself when we insist on having our *own way*. This is the heartbeat of a rebel against God. The humble response to any rebellion in our hearts is to confess it to God and forsake it (Proverbs 28:13). This *repentance* demonstrates one aspect of humility.

Our pride shows itself in a second way, however. Humility is also being aware that *someone else* is responsible for all that is good in our lives, including our successes. Pride is thinking that my own efforts and abilities are responsible for any accomplishments and successes.

1. Who are the people (give specific names) that God has placed in your life through the years who actually deserve credit for whatever positive things you see in your life today? (Hint: These would be family members, teachers, church leaders, etc. who have helped you in the past.)

   _____

   _____

   _____

   _____

   _____

2. Memorize 1 Peter 5:5 (Memory Card 15).

> *Likewise, ye younger, submit yourselves unto the elder. Yea, all of you be subject one to another, and be clothed with humility: for God resisteth the proud, and giveth grace to the humble.*

Being "clothed with humility" (1 Peter 5:5) is a concept that most of us very likely have never considered. We do not think of humility as a dominant characteristic of the contemporary "successful person." Today's athletes, entertainers, politicians, business people, and sadly, some church leaders are not known for their humility but for their self-confident arrogance, their control over others, and their self-indulgent lifestyles.

Our dislike for the whole idea of humility reveals how far off we are from understanding how life works in God's world.

3. Memorize Proverbs 14:12 (Memory Card 16).

> *There is a way which seemeth right unto a man, but the end thereof are the ways of death.*

4. In what areas of your life does God want you to stop fighting Him and to humbly surrender to Him?

_____

_____

_____

_____

_____

_____

To complete this checkpoint, you must read all the text, fill in the blanks, and memorize 1 Peter 5:5 and Proverbs 14:12.

☐ Text read.............................Date completed: _____ Initials: _____

☐ Blanks filled in ....Date completed: _____ Initials: _____

☐ 1 Peter 5:5 ....Date completed: _____ Initials: _____

☐ Proverbs 14:12...........................Date completed: _____ Initials: _____

I have completed Checkpoint 2.

Your name   Date

Group Leader's name   Date

CHECKPOINT 3 – HOW DOES GOD HUMBLE US?

God skillfully and lovingly can use the circumstances of our lives, or the choices we have made, or the choices others have made for us to help us turn in humility to him for help. In checkpoints 3-5, we want to look at four ways God uses our troubles to bring us to Him for the help we need.

First, God can use a problem we can't handle to expose our helplessness.

1. Read 2 Kings 5:1-15.

    ☐ Check the box when you finish reading the passage and then answer the following questions.

    • Could Naaman do anything to heal himself of the horrible, disfiguring, and, eventually, deadly disease of leprosy? _____

    • How did Naaman's pride manifest itself when he heard Elisha's instructions to dip in the river Jordan seven times?

    _____

    _____

45

- What happened when Naaman finally humbled himself and sought the solution God's way?

  _____

  _____

- Why would dipping in the river seven times be more humbling than dipping only one time?

  _____

  _____

- Naaman was cured of more than leprosy. What does the Bible say he learned in verse 15?

  _____

  _____

Like Namaan, we often come to God with an agenda of our own choosing. We think we know best what changes should occur in our lives and how those changes should be brought about. We believe that the blessings of life will be ours if we can just control the circumstances and people in our lives. The world around us continually tempts us to think that we can make life work on our own. God, however, can use those times when we have more than we can handle on our own to unravel our self-confidence. God has made us dependent by design and we must humble ourselves as Namaan did so that He can help us. *There can be no biblical change without humility.*

2. **Memorize Proverbs 3:5-6 (Memory Card 17).**

   Trust in the Lord with all thine heart; and lean not unto thine own understanding. In all thy ways acknowledge him, and he shall direct thy paths.

Second, God can give us a command we won't obey to expose our self-centeredness.

Another method of teaching humility is seen clearly in the account of Israel's prophet Jonah.[4] Jonah was popular in Israel at the time of the incidents described in the Old Testament book of Jonah. God knew the stubbornness of Jonah's heart, however, and set out to expose it. Perhaps a conversation like the following went on between Jonah and God.

A Rebel Prophet

"Jonah, I see you enjoy delivering messages of redemption to my people."

"Oh yes, Lord! You know how much I love to tell people about Your great deliverance on their behalf. That last assignment to the king about regaining the coastal country was a sheer delight. I love being Your messenger!"

"Good, Jonah, because I have a special message of redemption I want you to deliver to the Ninevites. I want to offer them salvation."

"But God, don't you know how brutal they are? Every group of people on earth hates them! They are barbaric! Why, when they bring their captives home from battle, they dismember them and make piles of their body parts outside their city gates just so show everyone that 'Ninevites rule!' and that 'Nobody messes with Ninevites!' Besides, they might do the same thing to me. They are awful people, Lord. They really deserve Your judgment. Besides, if I became an ambassador of good will to them, what will my fellow Israelites say? They will think I have betrayed them! I can't do this, God—this is asking too much!"

Although this conversation is made up, it captures the dynamics of Jonah's situation. God is commanding the prophet to show love to his neighbor by doing what his neighbor needs most. Jonah refuses, exposing his rebel heart. He runs.

---

[4]If you are not familiar with the story of Jonah, read the four short chapters in his book in the Old Testament.

47

Nineveh is due *east* of Palestine. Jonah gets on a ship headed for Tarshish, which is due *west* of Palestine. Tarshish is on the coast of Spain, which is the country farthest west in the then-known world. For all Jonah knew, the world dropped off on the other side of Tarshish.

Of course, it isn't long before God sends a great wind and shakes up the boat. The sailors finally throw Jonah overboard. God sends a great fish that swallows Jonah. After three days and nights in the fish's belly, Jonah surrenders to go to Nineveh, and the fish spits him up on shore.

Jonah makes the five-hundred-mile journey from Palestine to Nineveh and delivers God's message of judgment and redemption. To his disgust, the people repent—from the king down to the most humble beggar. Jonah is outraged! God has extended mercy to this city of barbarians who had terrorized the nations around them with their brutality. God has also exposed Jonah's selfish hatred.

When we insist upon our *own way*, God must humble us, as He did Jonah. *There can be no biblical change without humility.*

To complete this checkpoint, you must read all the text, fill in the blanks, and memorize Proverbs 3:5-6.

☐ Text read.......................Date completed: _____ Initials: _____

☐ Blanks filled in ....Date completed: _____ Initials: _____

☐ Proverbs 3:5-6.............Date completed: _____ Initials: _____

I have completed Checkpoint 3.

_____   _____
Your name   Date

_____   _____
Group Leader's name   Date

CHECKPOINT 4 –ANOTHER WAY GOD CAN HUMBLE US

Third, God can use an outcome we can't control to expose our sinfulness.

1. Read 2 Samuel 11:1-17 and 12:1-14.

    ☐ Check the box when you have read the passages.

It was shocking news to King David when he learned that his adultery with his neighbor's wife, Bathsheba, had resulted in her pregnancy. He had to do something! He murdered her husband and married her. But God was determined to expose David. When He did, David was humbled. Sin is pretty heady stuff. A man can start thinking that he can control the outcome of his sin. He thinks that he can get away with evil.

2. Write out Proverbs 28:13 in the blanks below.

    _____

    _____

    _____

    _____

    _____

Initially, David tried to cover his sins instead of repenting of them. When God determines to expose someone's sin, nothing that person can do can keep the sin hidden. Proverbs 28:13 is such a crucial verse for your Christian life. It is important that you memorize it and meditate upon what God says in the verse.

3. **Memorize Proverbs 28:13 (Memory Card 18).**

    He that covereth his sins shall not prosper: but whoso confesseth and forsaketh them shall have mercy.

4. Read Luke 15:11-24.

☐ Check the box when you have read the passage.

5. The wayward son described in this passage finally "came to himself" (v. 17). He realized that his sin must be confessed to and forgiven by two people. According to verse 18, who were those two people?

_____

_____

6. Ask yourself the following questions: Am I covering anything that needs to be resolved before God and others? Have I been totally honest in my dealings with others? Does what God knows about me differ from what others know about me? If so, describe what is happening.

_____

_____

_____

_____

_____

_____

Remember the statement from Unit One—"Not just any change will do." You cannot have biblical change on your own terms like Namaan or Jonah wanted. Neither can you have biblical change while you cover sin like King David did. *Humility—an awareness of your own neediness and of God's sufficiency—is the sign that shows you really understand life.* No man who sees how desperately he needs God in everything is self-confident, self-justifying, or self-protective. We are deceiving ourselves when we think that we do not need God or others. We were made, as we saw earlier in this unit, dependent by design. *Any change that will ultimately help a man must move him away from autonomy (self-rule and self-sufficiency) and dependence upon his Creator.*

To complete this checkpoint, you must read all the text, fill in the blanks, and memorize Proverbs 28:13.

☐ Text read...Date completed: _____ Initials: _____

☐ Blanks filled in ....Date completed: _____ Initials: _____

☐ Proverbs 28:13...........................Date completed: _____ Initials: _____

I have completed Checkpoint 4.

_____   _____
Your name   Date

_____   _____
Group Leader's name   Date

CHECKPOINT 5 – ONE MORE WAY GOD CAN HUMBLE US

Fourth, God can show that we can't understand everything to expose our limitations.

A certain man was the envy of every rancher in his part of Kansas. His cattle stock was some of the finest in the country, and his crops never failed to bring in bumper yields. Through the years he had become the wealthiest and most respected rancher in the area. Though he was rich, he never thought of himself as superior. In fact, because of his godliness, it was not unusual for him to spend an entire evening with a fellow rancher who needed personal advice about his family or who needed direction about a ranching decision. Then things changed!

In one evening, professional rustlers stole his entire stock in one section of the ranch, and a serious electrical storm started a fire on another part of the ranch, destroying the rest of his herd contained in the buildings. As if that weren't enough, the same electrical storm spawned a tornado that hit his oldest son's house, killing all the rancher's children, who had gathered there for a birthday celebration. The rancher and his wife had been delayed coming to the party, or they would have been killed too.

Of course, this account is fictional, but it is based upon the real-life experience of the Bible character Job. He too was known for his wisdom and wealth (Job 1:1-3). He too lost everything he had in one day (1:13-19). Shortly after his calamities, he also lost his health (2:1-10). Yet not until days later did he begin to question God and demand an explanation (23:1-17). He initially responded with unshakable faith in God. He said at the end of chapter 1, "Naked came I out of my mother's womb, and naked shall I return thither: the Lord gave, and the Lord hath taken away; blessed be the name of the Lord."

In chapter 3, Job begins to question why he was born, and in chapter 23, Job longs for a meeting with God to plead his case and to discover why he has endured this misery. Job's friends are little comfort to him. Job is not being tried because of his sin, as his friends suppose. His spiritual integrity is being tested by Satan—does he serve God for the personal gain he gets from God?

When enduring great pain, we, like Job, can begin to feel justified in our complaints against God and demand an explanation. We feel quite certain that God is entirely wrong in allowing this trouble to come our way.

1. What great difficulties are you experiencing that make life hard right now?

_____

_____

_____

_____

God answers Job, not with an explanation of the battle going on between Him and Satan but with a revelation in chapters 38-41 of the awesome power of the Almighty. God is very strong in His replies to Job. In essence, He says to Job, "Job, you need to get back in your place. If you think you are so smart and know better how to run this world, let's see how you do on a little quiz about how My world is governed. Tell me—if you have so much understanding. Have you walked on the bottom of the ocean, Job, and explored its depth? Have you ever made the sun rise in the morning? Do you know where I keep the treasuries of the ice and of the snow? Do you know how the stork brings forth her young in the right season?

For four chapters God questions Job about the universe around him, periodically asking him how he is doing on the "quiz". When presented with the awesome power and wisdom of God in the creation around him, Job takes the only action an honest man could do—he humbles himself.

Job was faced not just with circumstances he couldn't understand but with a God he could not comprehend. God exposed Job's finiteness—his limitations. As a creature, he could never understand the Almighty. In view of the awesome power and wisdom of his God, however, he could—and had to—trust Him. No other response is worthy of God. *The Almighty has made no mistake and deserves no rebuke. The creature cannot make demands of the Creator without revealing his arrogance.* God has made us dependent by design, and Job learned that the only proper response during the puzzling times of life is humility. There can be no biblical change without it.

What Is Your Next Step?

2. Is God dealing with your life in one of these ways? Is He trying to expose your lack of humility in the way you handle life? The first step back to God is repentance for going you *own way*. In light of what you have studied in this unit, describe what you know is the next step God wants you to take. If you have already taken that next step during this study, summarize it below.

_____

_____

_____

_____

_____

_____

3. Memorize John 12:24 (Memory Card 19).

Verily, verily, I say unto you, Except a corn of wheat fall into the ground and die, it abideth alone: but if it die, it bringeth forth much fruit.

4. Rememorize Luke 9:23-24 (Memory Card 20).

And he said to them all, If any man will come after me, let him deny himself, and take up his cross daily, and follow me. For whosoever will save his life shall lose it: but whosoever will lose his life for my sake, the same shall save it.

To complete this checkpoint, you must read all the text, fill in the blanks, memorize John 12:24, and rememorize Luke 9:23-24.

☐ Text read........................Date completed: _____ Initials: _____

☐ Blanks filled in ....Date completed: _____ Initials: _____

☐ John 12:24 ....Date completed: _____ Initials: _____

☐ Luke 9:23-24.............................Date completed: _____ Initials: _____

I have completed Checkpoint 5.

_____   _____
Your name   Date

_____   _____
Group Leader's name   Date

54

CHECKPOINT 6 – JOURNAL WORK

To complete this checkpoint you must journal ten days in a row.

I have completed Checkpoint 6.

_____   _____
Your name   Date

_____   _____
Group Leader's name   Date

CHECKPOINT 7 – CHURCH ATTENDANCE

To complete this checkpoint, you must do the following:

1. Attend two or more church services within one week. They can be the Sunday morning worship service, a Sunday school class, a Sunday evening service, or a midweek service (sometimes called "prayer meeting").

2. Fill in the information below, and have a pastor of the church sign the proper blank below.

Name of the church: _____

Check the services you attended:

☐ Sunday school

☐ Sunday morning worship service

☐ Sunday evening service

☐ Midweek service

☐ Other (explain): _____

Pastor's signature: _____

I have completed Checkpoint 7.

_____   _____
Your name   Date

_____   _____
Group Leader's name   Date

CHECKPOINT 8 – WRITTEN REPORT ON "HUMILITY"

To complete this checkpoint, write a one-page paper explaining the important truths you have learned in this lesson. To write the paper you will need to review your answers to remind yourself of what you have learned. Grammar and spelling are not an issue. Do the best you can, asking God to help you understand the importance of learning the process of how we grow and change.

I have completed Checkpoint 8.

_____   _____
Your name   Date

_____   _____
Group Leader's name   Date

CHECKPOINT 9 — SERVICE OPPORTUNITY

An important part of Christian living is serving God and others. To complete this checkpoint, you must ask your *Freedom That Lasts* director or your pastor to assign you some area of service for the church or for someone else. It may be an assignment to clean something at the church, to help someone with a special need, to help with setup for *Freedom That Lasts* classes, or to assist in some ministry of the church as a helper. In the blanks below, write out what you did at your pastor's or director's request.

_____

_____

_____

_____

I have completed Checkpoint 9.

_____   _____
Your name   Date

_____   _____
Group Leader's name   Date

CONGRATULATIONS!

You have completed the nine checkpoints necessary to finish this unit. The road map towards growth and change into Christlikeness should be clearer to you now.

When you finish all the checkpoints for this unit and your group leader has signed off on them, you will receive your reward at the end of that class. We encourage you to invite your friends and family to witness your accomplishment.

If you will continue the lessons in this book and faithfully use your *Spiritual Life Journal,* you will come to know your God much, much better than you do now!

UNIT 4

SELF-DENIAL

> For if ye live after the flesh, ye shall die: but if ye through the Spirit do mortify the deeds of the body, ye shall live.
> Romans 8:13

CHECKPOINT 1 – MORTIFYING A MOTORCYCLE

My father, my two brothers, and I were all avid motorcyclists when I was growing up. Although the combined miles traveled by the four of us would be quite high, I was the only one to have a serious accident.

On the day of my accident I was cruising along at a modest speed on a country two-lane highway near our home. A South Dakota tornado had devastated the area. My passenger, Randy, and I were looking over the damage. My attention was drawn to a demolished farm equipment dealership on the left side of the road. I did not notice the pickup that had stopped in my lane just yards ahead of me. The driver was waiting for a break in traffic in the oncoming lane so that he could turn left into the dealership. I noticed him just a split second before I slammed into his tailgate going thirty miles per hour!

I woke up a few minutes later with a badly mangled bike, multiple fractures to my right wrist, and damage to my neck. I had flipped over into the pickup bed and landed on the back of my head. Had I not been wearing a helmet—a requirement of Dad's—I would have been dead. Randy, of course, followed me into the pickup bed and landed on top of me. He walked away without a scratch.

Had I seen the pickup a few seconds earlier, I probably could have avoided the accident. Stopping a motorcycle involves combining three actions in various ways, depending upon the circumstances.

1. Let up on the hand-throttle to cut down on the amount of fuel to the engine.

2. Apply the brakes to reduce forward motion.

3. Disengage the clutch with the foot pedal to prohibit the engine's power from driving the rear wheel.

Had I had enough time to initiate these actions at the time of my accident, I would have "put to death"—stopped—the force of the engine that was propelling me to destruction. I would have been able to stop all forward motion and come to a resting stop a few feet behind the pickup. The engine would have been still idling, but because of the combination of actions listed above, all of its ability to ruin me would have been "put to death." If I were using Elizabethan terms, like those found in the King James Version of the Bible, I could say that I had "mortified my motorcycle" or more specifically, "mortified my motorcycle's forward motion."

Today we use the word *mortify* only to indicate a strong measure of embarrassment. We might say, "When Joe told that story about me, I was mortified. I could have died!" The apostle Paul uses the word translated *mortify*, however, to indicate a process of "deadening" the power of the flesh. Literally he meant that we are to "drain the life out of" the flesh through the Holy Spirit's assistance.

1. **Rememorize Romans 8:13 (Memory Card 21).**

    For if ye live after the flesh, ye shall die: but if ye through the Spirit do mortify the deeds of the body, ye shall live.

2. Read Romans 6.

    ☐ Check the box when you have finished reading it.

3. Romans 6:22 summarizes Romans 6. What does it say about the ability of sin to influence us if we are mortifying the flesh?

We are "made _____ from sin,
and become _____ to God."

Romans 6 is such an important chapter in understanding how to battle your flesh that you will be re-memorizing several verses from that chapter in this unit.

4. Take time right now to identify the battles you are facing at the present time. You need to have specific struggles of the flesh in mind as you work through this unit. The list could include such sins as worry, deception, destructive bodily habits (such as drugs, cutting, drinking, anorexia, bulimia, or overeating), anger, a critical spirit, gossip, a complaining spirit, profanity and other sins of the tongue, bitterness, laziness, pride, rebellion to authorities in your life, greed and materialism, gambling, or immoral behavior (such as lustful fantasies, pornography, adultery, or homosexuality), and so forth. Write them in the blanks below. Of course, the more personal sins—especially immorality—you would not write down for others to see if they found your book. The main idea to remember is that all these sinful activities and actions can be changed, as we shall see in this study.

_____

_____

_____

_____

_____

_____

_____

5. **Memorize Romans 6:6 (Memory Card 22).**

> *Knowing this, that our old man is crucified with him, that the body of sin might be destroyed, that henceforth we should not serve sin.*

NOTE: The phrase "old man" refers to what we were "in Adam" before our salvation. The phrase "the body of sin" refers to the totality of us under the absolute rule of our sinful nature before we became children of God. The word *destroyed* means "brought to nothing" or drained of its absolute power.

6. **Memorize Romans 6:9-12 (Memory Card 23).**

> *Knowing that Christ being raised from the dead dieth no more; death hath no more dominion over him. For in that he died, he died unto sin once: but in that he liveth, he liveth unto God. Likewise reckon ye also yourselves to be dead indeed unto sin, but alive unto God through Jesus Christ our Lord. Let not sin therefore reign in your mortal body, that ye should obey it in the lusts thereof.*

To complete this checkpoint, you must read all the text, fill in the blanks, memorize Romans 8:13, Romans 6:6, and rememorize Romans 6:9-12.

☐ Text read....................................Date completed: _____ Initials: _____

☐ Blanks filled in ....Date completed: _____ Initials: _____

☐ Romans 8:13 ....Date completed: _____ Initials: _____

☐ Romans 6:6.................................Date completed: _____ Initials: _____

☐ Romans 6:9-12 ....Date completed: _____ Initials: _____

I have completed Checkpoint 1.

Your name   Date

Group Leader's name   Date

CHECKPOINT 2 – TO MORTIFY YOUR FLESH YOU HAVE TO *KNOW* SOME THINGS

To stop my motorcycle I need to know some things. Knowing how to apply the brakes is helpful, but braking is only a part of the stopping process. There are other facts I need to know—such as how to disengage the engine using the clutch and how to cut the fuel to the engine to slow it down. I could be in big trouble if I don't *know* these things or if I don't *apply* them.

Romans 6 deals with an important doctrine[5] of the Christian walk. Bible teachers have called this doctrine by various names, the most common being our "union with Christ" or our "identification with Christ." Perhaps you have tried to stop your addiction or harmful habit by sheer willpower and self-discipline but have been unsuccessful. The reason you failed is that trying to resist the flesh without *knowing* and *applying* this basic doctrine is like trying to stop a speeding motorcycle by putting on the brakes while leaving the clutch engaged and the engine running full throttle.

The motorcycle brakes eventually overheat and give out—like your willpower does. The power of the engine must be disconnected from the wheel assembly. Its connection must be "broken" so that it no longer influences the motorcycle's forward motion to destruction.

In a similar fashion, Christ has made a way that the pull of indwelling sin can be broken so that it does not have to affect the way we live. Before our salvation, we had no choice but to obey the sinful pulls within. It was as if we were riding a motorcycle without a clutch.

---

[5] The word *doctrine* simply means "teaching." Our God is a God of truth, and He calls His truth "doctrine."

The engine was always running, and the wheels were always turning. There was no way to disconnect the engine. The back wheel was a "slave" to the engine. It had to turn when the engine turned.

Romans 6 teaches us, however, that because of Christ's death and resurrection, we have been "made free from sin" (6:22). We no longer *have* to obey its pull to go our *own way*. How is that possible? Answer the question below and then pay close attention to the rest of the explanation in this checkpoint. *Follow Paul's teaching carefully because this is an especially important doctrine in breaking the power of sin in your life.*

1. Before salvation, what was the only response we could have to the pull of indwelling sin within us?

   _____

   _____

Paul says in Romans 6:3 that "so many of us as were baptized into *his* death." "Baptism" here is not referring to the church ordinance of water baptism. That is our public testimony of new life *after* salvation. Rather, Romans 6:3 is referring to what the Holy Spirit does for us *at the moment* of our salvation. The word *baptize* means to "place into" or "immerse."

Paul says here that we are "immersed" or included in all the activities of Christ's death, burial, and resurrection.

That means that when He died, *we* died. When He was buried, *we* were buried. When He rose from the dead, *we* were raised, to "walk in newness of life" (Romans 6:4). Verse 6 says "*Knowing* this [remember, Paul wants us to *know* something], that our old man is crucified with him, that the body of sin might be destroyed [its absolute power put to death], that henceforth we should not serve sin."

Before our identification with Christ in this way, we, in these earthly bodies, were *required* to serve the flesh. If our sinful bent was better served by lusting, we lusted. If it was better served by lying, we lied. We were truly "servants to sin" (Romans 6:20). Paul tells us, however, that the control of that indwelling sin over us has been destroyed or "nullified."

We can choose to obey the impluses of our sinful nature—our flesh—if we want to, but we don't have to give in any longer. *Christ has freed us from the flesh's absolute control that it had before we were saved.*

But Do You Know How to *Fix* Your Motorcycle?

My dad wanted us not only to know how to *ride* our motorcycles but also to *understand how they worked* so that we could get the most enjoyment and use out of them. I'll have to admit that riding a motorcycle seemed a lot more fun than troubleshooting an ignition failure or a carburetor problem. A good friend owned a motorcycle identical to mine, but he didn't even know which end of a screwdriver to hold in his hand and which end went into the screw! He was always frustrated with himself and his bike because he didn't know how to detect when something was going wrong—like when his clutch cable was getting loose. When it created a problem for him, he didn't know how to fix it. Consequently, I spent a lot of time fixing his bike for him.

In the same way, you may find the paragraphs you are studying in this unit *very* hard to understand and *very* long—in fact, this is the "heaviest" and the longest unit in the entire study! Many Christians try to enjoy their Christian life but are frequently frustrated and defeated because they can't detect when something is going wrong until it is too late, and then they don't know how to fix it. *If you will ask God to make the truths in this unit clear to you, you will have mastered one of the most important truths you can know in the Christian life.* If you skim over this material, you will be just one more frustrated and failing Christian. So hang in there! You need to *know* this!

Lessons from a Funeral Home

During my first year of marriage, I worked in a funeral home. I assisted the drivers as they picked up the bodies from the morgue or from a nursing home and then helped later with the family visitation times. The loved ones of the deceased—most of whom were not believers—despaired because the deceased no longer responded to them. No matter how much they cried or grieved, he would not speak to them, hold their hands, or try to comfort them in any way—he was dead! His power to respond was destroyed.

This is the picture Paul wants us to have in Romans 6—dead people don't respond! We no longer have to respond to the pull of the flesh within because sin's absolute power over us died when Christ died. *We are to consider ourselves dead to sin.* We now have a choice! We are free from sin's absolute rule—its "dominion." We are now free to respond to the Holy Spirit, who lives in us. We will not only "live with him" (6:8) in heaven later, but we can also experience a "newness of life" now (6:4).

2. In what areas of life do you know God wants you to be dead to the pull of your flesh?

_____

_____

_____

_____

_____

_____

Lessons from the Landlord

To illustrate this further, let's say that you have been renting a home from a man named Mr. Brown. On the first day of every month he comes to your door to collect the rent. This month Mr. Brown sold the home to Mr. Smith. To your surprise, when the rent is due next month, Mr. Brown shows up at your door again to collect the rent. In months past you were *required* to pay Mr. Brown. You were under his "power." When he sold the house, however, his power to collect the rent was broken. You can pay him if you want, but you don't have to. You are now *required* to pay the new landlord, Mr. Smith.

3. Mr. Smith is the new landlord. Mr. Brown begs you to pay him. Do you have to pay Mr. Brown? _____
Why or why not?

_____

_____

_____

In the same way, we are no longer *required* to obey the flesh. "For [indwelling] sin shall not have dominion [control] over you" (Romans 6:14). Your life is under new management. You are no longer under the power of sin. A new "landlord" has taken over. A new set of requirements from a new Lord is in place—the law of God (Romans 7:25). You are a servant to a new master.

4. Do you have to obey the flesh? _____ Why or why not?

_____

_____

_____

_____

_____

Paul says, "This is something you need to *know!*" Resisting the temptation to return to your harmful habit, addiction, or negative thought patters starts here. As I mentioned earlier, you cannot stop a motorcycle by merely applying the brakes. Your "brakes" of self-discipline will give out. The strain will be too much. Your endurance will eventually give out, and you will crash anyway. You have to *know* this if you are going to "mortify your motorcycle"—kill its forward motion toward destruction. In the next checkpoint we will look at how to *apply* the truths you have seen in this checkpoint.

5. According to what you have learned in this lesson, what is the reason you no longer "have to" obey the temptations of indwelling sin?

_____

_____

_____

_____

6. Rememorize Romans 6:13-14 (Memory Card 24).

> *Neither yield ye your members as instruments of unrighteousness unto sin: but yield yourselves unto God, as those that are alive from the dead, and your members as instruments of righteousness unto God. For sin shall not have dominion over you: for ye are not under the law, but under grace.*

To complete this checkpoint, you must read all the text, fill in the blanks, and rememorize Romans 6:13-14.

☐ Text read......................................Date completed: _____ Initials: _____

☐ Blanks filled in ....Date completed: _____ Initials: _____

☐ Romans 6:13-14........................Date completed: _____ Initials: _____

I have completed Checkpoint 2.

Your name _____   Date _____

Group Leader's name _____   Date _____

CHECKPOINT 3 – TO MORTIFY THE FLESH YOU HAVE TO '*RECKON*' SOME THINGS

After the apostle Paul in Romans 6 finishes telling us the facts we need to *know* about our union with Christ, he begins explaining to us the implications of those facts in Romans 6:11. He says, "Likewise reckon ye also yourselves to be dead indeed unto sin, but alive unto God through Jesus Christ our Lord." Paul is saying, "God knows you have been freed from the requirements to obey indwelling sin. Now *you* need to take it personally and quit living as if you *had* to obey it; start living unto God."

1. Fill in the blanks from the sentences in the previous paragraph.

"_____ knows you have been freed
from the _____ to
_____ indwelling sin. Now
_____ need to take it personally and
quite living as if you _____ to obey it."

We need to understand that if we pay Mr. Brown, we choose to do so.
We may have grown used to the previous landlord and his ways. We
may have felt the rent was too much at times and that his demands
were unpleasant, but we were bound by law to pay him. The *fact*,
however, is that our house is under new management. We must now
reckon that to be true, *"Reckon" here means to "consider" it to be true for
us.*

Lessons from a Speed Limit Sign

We "reckon" things every day. When we drive along the highway, we
see a speed limit sign that says "speed limit 55." We are expected to
"reckon," or consider, that sign to be binding for us. *We are to apply
it to our lives.* We are to believe that it is an accurate statement of the
government's expectations on that highway and that it applies to us.
That is an act of *faith*. If we don't *believe* the reality of the law and
our accountability to it, we will be reminded of that with a speeding
ticket. We will be held accountable for not "reckoning" it to be true
for us. Paul says, "God reckons it to be true, and you *likewise* need to
reckon yourself to be dead indeed unto sin." You do not have to obey
its urges and pulls.

But I Don't Feel Like It!

You may protest, however, "I don't *feel* free. When those sinful
impulses arise in my heart, I *feel* as though I *have* to obey!" You
are going to have to take it by faith then that these facts are true
no matter how you feel. It may *feel* as though you *have* to give in,
but you need to *know* better because God said otherwise. You must
consider yourself to be "dead *indeed* unto sin" (Romans 6:11).

Many people fail right here. They make decisions about what they
will or will not do based upon how they *feel* at the moment—not by

the *facts* of what God has said is reality. They don't consider things to be true because God says they are true. They consider a thing to be true only if it feels to them as though it might be true. The result of this kind of living is instability. They are "up and down," moody, and unpredictable.

This is the kind of man James describes as a double-minded man. He is "minding" the flesh and his feelings one moment and then "minding" God and His truth the next. James says he is "like a wave of the sea driven with the wind and tossed" (1:6) and warns, "let not that man think that he shall receive anything of the Lord. A double-minded man is unstable in all his ways" (1:7-8).

2. According to the previous paragraph, what does it mean to be double-minded?

_____

_____

_____

_____

You cannot afford to let your ways be determined by the twisted view of reality that your flesh and its feelings will give you. We no longer have to fulfill those desires—those *feelings* of our flesh and of our mind. *Don't give into those feelings that are generated by fleshly, selfish thinking. They will not give you an accurate picture of reality. They will keep you trapped in a fantasy world of make-believe. You must "reckon" yourselves "dead indeed unto sin."*

3. Do you see yourself in the double-minded man who is inconsistent, up and down spiritually, perhaps moody and unpredictable because he is not faithfully reckoning himself "dead indeed unto sin" (Romans 6:11)? If so, in what ways does this show up in your personal and public life?

_____

_____

_____

_____

_____

Not only must we *know* some things that are facts about our identification with Christ in His death, burial, and resurrection and *reckon* those things to be true for us, but as Paul tells us, we must also *yield* to the right master as a result of what we *know* and *reckon*. We will look in the next checkpoint at what it means to "yield [ourselves] unto God" (Romans 6:13).

4. Memorize Romans 8:12-13 (Memory Card 25).

> *Therefore, brethren, we are debtors, not to the flesh, to live after the flesh. For if ye live after the flesh, ye shall die: but if ye through the Spirit do mortify the deeds of the body, ye shall live.*

5. Memorize 1 Corinthians 15:57-58 (Memory Card 26).

> *But thanks be to God, which giveth us the victory through our Lord Jesus Christ. Therefore, my beloved brethren, be ye stedfast, unmoveable, always abounding in the work of the Lord, forasmuch as ye know that your labour is not in vain in the Lord.*

To complete this checkpoint, you must read all the text, fill in the blanks, memorize Romans 8:12-13 and 1 Corinthians 15:57-58.

☐ Text read......................................Date completed: _____ Initials: _____

☐ Blanks filled in ....Date completed: _____ Initials: _____

☐ Romans 8:12-13 ....Date completed: _____ Initials: _____

☐ 1 Corinthians 15:57-58 ....Date completed: _____ Initials: _____

I have completed Checkpoint 3.

Your name   Date

Group Leader's name   Date

CHECKPOINT 4 – TO MORTIFY THE FLESH YOU HAVE TO *YIELD* SOME THINGS

You might again find yourself at this point protesting and saying, "I'm not good at yielding. That comes hard for me. I'm not sure I know how to yield." Paul reminds us in Romans, however that we are all experts at "yielding." We have done it for years—only to the wrong master. We are skilled at yielding our bodily "members as instruments [weapons] of unrighteousness unto sin" (6:13)—addictions, harmful habits and thinking patters. We therefore know what it is like to be "servants of sin" (6:17). The result of this yielding to sin is the "things whereof ye are now ashamed" and whose "end … is death" (6:21).

After Paul reminds us that we have had much practice yielding to a master, he says, "As ye have yielded your members servants to uncleanness and to iniquity unto iniquity [from one level of sin to the next]; even so now yield your members servants to righteousness unto holiness" (6:19). The result will be "fruit unto holiness, and the end everlasting life" (6:22).

So we are now at a point of decision about how we will respond to whatever pull the flesh has on us at the moment. Are we going to deny God—say no to Him—or deny the impulses of our sinful nature? Are we going to walk after the flesh or walk after the Spirit? Are we going to obey God or obey indwelling sin? The choice to obey God (yielding) is a twofold responsibility. We will look at one aspect in this checkpoint and look at the other in the final checkpoint in this unit.

1. Some people say, "I'm just not good at yielding. That comes hard for me. I'm not sure I know how to yield." What is wrong with this protest? Back up your answer with specific examples.

_____

_____

_____

_____

Don't Obey the Flesh!

We would like to think that in this or that sin, we have been *defeated*. The humbling reality is that we have been *disobedient*. The battle can be expressed as simply as this:

Just two choices on the shelf—pleasing God or pleasing self[6]

The Christian life is not an easy life because of this warring sinfulness that dwells within us. Though it isn't easy, it isn't complicated. Complications are usually the natural consequences of going our *own way*. But even at that, the way out of those complications is always a series of *simple* choices: "In this thing or that thing before me, am I going to please God or please my own sinful desires?"

2. Complete the sentences from the previous paragraph.

   • "Complications are usually the natural
     _____ of going our
     _____ _____."

   • "The way out of those complications
     is _____ a series of
     _____ choices."

Paul defined the kind of yielding we are to do as *obeying*. He says, "Know ye not, that to whom ye yield yourselves servants to obey, his servants ye are to whom ye obey; whether of sin unto death, or of obedience unto righteousness? But God be thanked, that ye *were* the

_____

[6]Ken Collier, THE WILDS Christian Association. Used by permission.

servants of sin, but *ye have obeyed* from the heart that form of doctrine [teaching] which was delivered you" (Romans 6:16-17).

Don't miss the point here. Paul does not prescribe some long, complicated series of therapy steps. He says, "You got yourself into this mess by obeying your flesh and denying God, and the only way out is to start denying the flesh and obeying God." Paul is clear—the flesh *can* be denied, and it *must* be denied! This is the path to victory.

3. The opening paragraph in this section, "Don't Obey the Flesh!" says, "We would like to think that in this or that sin, we have been *defeated*. The humbling reality is that we have been *disobedient.*"

   • Do you agree with this statement?

     _____

   • Give your reasons for agreeing or disagreeing with the statement.

     _____

     _____

     _____

     _____

     _____

     _____

Let me illustrate the truths we have been discussing with a real-life example of a young man I'll call Kirk.

A Lesson from Kirk

Kirk was a twenty-five-year old shipping clerk for a local truck line. He came for help about his continual tardiness to work in the mornings. He was consistently thirty minutes late. His boss appreciated the high level of competence and commitment Kirk demonstrated on the job but was growing increasingly frustrated by Kirk's late arrivals. Kirk had been given a verbal job warning and knew he must take action about his habitual failure in this area.

Kirk told me that he set his alarm clock each morning for half past six and that it awakened him every morning. He said that he had even placed the clock on the dresser across the room so that he would have to get out of bed and walk across the room to turn off the alarm.

Kirk revealed with great embarrassment, however, that once he had turned off the alarm, he went back to bed. He would sleep until about half past seven and then make a frantic attempt to arrive at work by eight o'clock. Of course, he never made it on time.

I asked him, "Kirk, on the way from the alarm clock back to your bed, do you ever get under conviction from God about staying up instead of going back to bed?" Kirk replied, "Oh yes! Every day while I shuffle back to the bed I am convicted about it. God reminds me that I should not go back to bed."

I asked him pointedly, "Kirk, if I come to your apartment for the next couple of weeks, awaken you at half past six and tell you to stay up, will you stay up?" Kirk's face became very serious as he assured me that if I were to awaken him and tell him to stay up, he would do it. He would not let me down if I tried to help him in this way. I then pointed out to Kirk the real issue. He had just revealed that if *I* spoke to him he would stay up, but if *God* spoke to him he would go back to bed.

The important issue to see here is that what we often call a lack of self-discipline is actually a lack of *obedience* to God. This should be familiar ground to you because in the first student manual you learned the definition of self-control:

Instantly obeying God's Word in the power of God's Spirit

That definition captures this important lesson. *God's Spirit is at work convicting and leading, but we often aren't obeying.* I told Kirk that if he wanted to become disciplined in this area, he needed to let the Holy Spirit "disciple" him. *If he would obey God's Spirit, he would end up being a disciplined person.*

This is what Paul meant when he spoke about *yielding*. Instead of obeying the flesh's cry to postpone responsibility, Kirk needed to obey the Holy Spirit's conviction to resist the flesh.

4. Complete the sentence from the paragraphs above.

    "What we often call a lack of_____
    is actually a lack of _____ to
    God."

5. In this story about Kirk, you learned that after he turned off the alarm, he went back to bed. He admitted that every day God convicted him and reminded him not to go back to bed.

    *   Are there similar issues in your life for which God convicts you again and again? _____

    *   If so, what are they?

        _____

        _____

        _____

        _____

        _____

6. **Rememorize Romans 6:16-18 (Memory Card 27).**

    Know ye not, that to whom ye yield yourselves servants to obey, his servants ye are to whom ye obey; whether of sin unto death, or of obedience unto righteousness? But God be thanked, that ye were the servants of sin, but ye have obeyed from the heart that form of doctrine which was delivered you. Being then made free from sin, ye became the servants of righteousness.

7. Memorize Romans 6:19 (Memory Card 28).

For as ye have yielded your members servants to uncleanness and to iniquity unto iniquity; even so now yield your members servants to righteousness unto holiness.

To complete this checkpoint, you must read all the text, fill in the blanks, rememorize Romans 6:16-18, and memorize Romans 6:19.

☐ Text read......................................Date completed: _____ Initials: _____

☐ Blanks filled in ....Date completed: _____ Initials: _____

☐ Romans 6:16-18.........................Date completed: _____ Initials: _____

☐ Romans 6:19 ....Date completed: _____ Initials: _____

I have completed Checkpoint 4.

Your name   Date

Group Leader's name   Date

CHECKPOINT 5 – MORE LESSONS FROM KIRK

Don't Feed the Flesh!

In the last checkpoint we saw our first lesson from Kirk: "Don't obey the flesh!" In this checkpoint we will see that because Kirk was *feeding* the flesh, it was easy for him to *obey* the flesh.

Although Kirk needed to obey God's Spirit instead of his flesh in the morning alarm clock routine, further questioning into Kirk's lifestyle revealed other, more serious matters. When I asked Kirk about his evening schedule, he told me that in addition to his eight-hour day job, he also worked an evening part-time job until half past nine. After work he would go out for coffee with a couple of his coworkers and arrive home about eleven o'clock.

Since he felt he owed himself a little pleasure to make up for the day's "rat race," he would usually watch a movie for another couple of hours. Usually the movie was filled with violence and immorality. He would often fall asleep on the couch and drag himself to bed when the movie was over about one o'clock. You can now understand why getting up at half past six was hard for Kirk. A major cause of his early morning struggle to get out of bed was obviously the fatigued state of his body, but the effect of his lifestyle on his soul was even more destructive. *Kirk was feeding his flesh in several ways throughout his daily routine and then was discouraged because he could not overcome his flesh in the morning.*

To begin with, his soul was worn down daily by the wickedness of the people around him at work. He was daily exposed to ungodly attitudes, conversation, values, and temptations. Like Lot, his soul was "vexed" (literally, worn down or tortured) "from day to day with their unlawful deeds" (2 Peter 2:7-8). God is clear in this passage that a believer who is exposed to the "filthy conversation [sensual lifestyle] of the wicked" will be worn down as he is "seeing and hearing" their "unlawful deeds."

If the believer is exercising his will *against* these influences, he is not nearly as affected by them. *If, however, he is at all passive to these influences, the result is clear—he will be worn down!* Kirk never witnessed to his lost coworkers and never walked away from their shameless, sensual talk. He never resisted the evil around him in any way.

Since Kirk was in a weakened spiritual condition, he was not enjoying fellowship with God and constantly felt guilty about his walk with the Lord. Consequently, his work was not a source of joy to him. Rather than clocking out at the end of the shift satisfied that he had done his best for Christ that day and grateful for the opportunities for spiritual witness, he was constantly reminded of his disobedience in promptness and witness.

The conversations at the coffee shop after work would always drag him down further. He would return home feeling very guilty for his participation in their filthy talk. Not wanting to go to bed feeling so down, he would watch a movie. Usually the movie was filled with profanity, adult themes, or violence. Of course, feeding his flesh in this way destroyed any hope of resisting its pull in such a small matter as getting out of bed in the morning.

Cut the Fuel!

I think the picture here is clear for us. If you wish to restrain the flesh as God commands, you are being foolish to feed it. Peter warned earlier, "Abstain from fleshly lusts, which war against the soul" (1 Peter 2:11). We have to exercise self-denial by saying no to the pull of the flesh in the area we are working on, but we also have to say no to the *any* pull to feed the flesh, thus making it stronger. Every time we feed it in one area of life, we make it harder to say no to it in *any* area. Its pull and control become stronger.

Like the motorcycle we are trying to "mortify," it is no use to merely put on the brakes; we must cut the fuel to the engine. Most believers forget they have a "clutch"—they don't *have* to obey the flesh—and try to stop the bike with the brakes while feeding more fuel to the engine. Cut the fuel! Even then, since the flesh is always with us this side of heaven, the engine never stops. At best it is idling; at worst it is racing!

1. **Rememorize Galatians 6:7-9 (Memory Card 29).**

    Be not deceived; God is not mocked: for whatsoever a man soweth, that shall he also reap. For he that soweth to his flesh shall of the flesh reap corruption; but he that soweth to the Spirit shall of the Spirit reap life everlasting. And let us not be weary in well doing: for in due season we shall reap, if we faint not.

A "Flesh-Free" Diet

Many in our society who are watching their weight try to eat low-fat foods. They can even become obsessed with counting fat grams of intake and measuring calories burned in exercise. To paraphrase a Scripture text, their life motto could be "Make no provision for fattening foods lest ye put on the weight thereof."

Oh, that there were even a fraction of that kind of concern in believers to be living "flesh-free"—as much as possible in the world! We are told to "make [no] provision [thinking ahead of time that leads into indulgence] for the flesh, to fulfill the lusts thereof" (Romans 13:14). Yet our Christian society consumes the world's entertainment and philosophies and embraces its goals and attitudes; consequently, Christians like Kirk are powerless to make any impact for God upon the world around them.

2. **Memorize Romans 13:14 (Memory Card 30).**

    But put ye on the Lord Jesus Christ, and make not provision for the flesh, to fulfill the lusts thereof.

The Seat Belt of Self-Denial

As we have seen, the Bible calls this restraint *denying self*—saying no to what your sinful flesh wants you to do. Jesus said in Luke 9:23, "If any man will come after me, let him deny himself." Like a seat belt, the restraint of self-denial protects us from danger. A seat belt helps protect us from bodily injury if we are involved in an accident.

Self-denial protects us from the danger of giving in to the urges of the flesh. A seat belt, to be effective, must be worn anytime we are riding in a car. We are never too young or too old to wear a seat belt. Age has nothing to do with its necessity. *A seat belt is always needed because the danger is always present.*

In the same way, we are never too old to be practicing self-denial. Since the flesh is always with us, *self-denial is always needed because the danger is always present.*

3. **Memorize Psalm 139:23-24 (Memory Card 31).**

    Search me, O God, and know my heart: try me, and know my thoughts: and see if there be any wicked way in me, and lead me in the way everlasting.

4. Take some time to answer the following questions about your schedule and lifestyle. Make Psalm 139:23-24 your prayer as you rate yourself on each item below and prayerfully consider the amount of fleshly influence in your life. Use the following scale to rate yourself.

1=mostly high in "flesh content"

2=somewhat high in "flesh content"

3=seldom high in "flesh content"

4=never high in "flesh content"

- Is your entertainment flesh-free? Rate

    _____ the *content* of the movies and television programs you watch

    _____ the *style* and *content* of the music you listen to

    _____ the *atmosphere* of your favorite restaurants or places you hang out

    _____ the *values* you absorb watching or participating in your favorite sports

    _____ the amount of *time* you spend in these kinds of pursuits

- Is your pursuit of possessions flesh-free (clothes, electronics, cars, etc.)? Rate

    _____ the appeal to your *pride* in being accepted with the group you wish to impress

    _____ the *stumbling-block* you are to others who are trying to impress you the same way

    _____ the *sexual appeal* to others in the way you dress

    _____ the *values* you absorb when studying the latest fashions, lifestyle, sports, and consumer websites and magazines to make sure you are current

- Are your friendships flesh-free? Rate

    _____ the *content* of your conversation—sexual, crude, materialistic, or obsessive _____the physical *contact* with others—arousing sexual desires in them and in you that cannot righteously be gratified

_____the "iron sharpening iron" *influence* on each other for godliness (living as though God is all that matters) or for worldliness ("living as though the world—*our* world—is all that matters")[7]

_____the *attitudes* that are fostered—authority versus rebellion, order versus chaos and disorder, and so forth

How then do you weaken the flesh? How do you mortify it?

Cut the fuel to the flesh "engine" by not feeding the flesh. *Disengage the clutch*—remind yourself that the engine doesn't have to drive the wheel. The power of indwelling sin has been overruled by Christ—reckon it to be so for you. Lastly, *put on the brakes.* Deny self! Say no to the flesh.

To complete this checkpoint, you must read all the text, fill in the blanks, rememorize Galatians 6:7-9, and memorize Romans 13:14 and Psalm 139:23-24.

☐ Text read....................................Date completed: _____ Initials: _____

☐ Blanks filled in ....Date completed: _____ Initials: _____

☐ Galatians 6:7-9...........................Date completed: _____ Initials: _____

☐ Romans 13:14............................Date completed: _____ Initials: _____

☐ Psalm 139:23-24 ....Date completed: _____ Initials: _____

---

[7] Erwin W. Lutzer, *How in This World Can I Be Holy?* (Chicago: Moody Press, 1974), 26. Italics are Lutzer's.

I have completed Checkpoint 5.

Your name   Date

Group Leader's name   Date

CHECKPOINT 6 – JOURNAL WORK

To complete this checkpoint you must journal ten days in a row.

I have completed Checkpoint 6.

Your name   Date

Group Leader's name   Date

CHECKPOINT 7 – CHURCH ATTENDANCE

To complete this checkpoint, you must do the following:

1. Attend two or more church services within one week. They can be the Sunday morning worship service, a Sunday school class, a Sunday evening service, or a midweek service (sometimes called "prayer meeting").

2. Fill in the information below, and have a pastor of the church sign the proper blank below.

   Name of the church: _____

   Check the services you attended:

☐ Sunday school

☐ Sunday morning worship service

☐ Sunday evening service

☐ Midweek service

☐ Other (explain): _____

Pastor's signature: _____

I have completed Checkpoint 7.

Your name	Date
Group Leader's name	Date

CHECKPOINT 8 – WRITTEN REPORT ON "SELF-DENIAL"

To complete this checkpoint, write a one-page paper explaining the important truths you have learned in this lesson. To write the paper you will need to review your answers to remind yourself of what you have learned. Grammar and spelling are not an issue. Do the best you can, asking God to help you understand the importance of learning the process of how we grow and change.

I have completed Checkpoint 8.

Your name	Date
Group Leader's name	Date

CHECKPOINT 9 — SERVICE OPPORTUNITY

An important part of Christian living is serving God and others. To complete this checkpoint, you must join your church's visitation group one time and go with an experienced soulwinner to give the gospel to someone and invite that person to church. Or you can ask your pastor or *Freedom That Lasts* director to connect you with an experienced believer who will take you with him looking for someone to give the gospel to. In the blanks below tell who you went with, summarize what the two of you did, and discuss what you learned.

_____

_____

_____

_____

_____

_____

_____

_____

_____

_____

_____

_____

_____

_____

_____

_____

I have completed Checkpoint 9.

```
_____        _____
Your name                      Date


_____        _____
Group Leader's name            Date
```

CONGRATULATIONS!

You have completed the nine checkpoints necessary to finish this unit. The road map towards growth and change into Christlikeness should be clearer to you now.

When you finish all the checkpoints for this unit and your group leader has signed off on them, you will receive your reward at the end of that class. We encourage you to invite your friends and family to witness your accomplishment.

If you will continue the lessons in this book and faithfully use your *Spiritual Life Journal,* you will come to know your God much, much better than you do now!

UNIT 5

KNOWING GOD

> Abide in me, and I in you. As the branch cannot bear fruit of itself, except it abide in the vine; no more can ye, except ye abide in me. I am the vine, ye are the branches: He that abideth in me, and I in him, the same bringeth forth much fruit: for without me ye can do nothing.
> (John 15:4-5)

CHECKPOINT 1 – UNDERSTANDING THE REAL WORLD

If the *own way* tendency of indwelling sin, as we have seen in the last three units, is our real problem, what then is the real solution? We ought to be convinced by now that the solution does not lie within us. We are the problem—not the solution!

The world says and, sadly, many Christians say that Bible solutions will not work in the "real" world. The irony of their complaint is that the Bible *alone* gives the only true picture of the "real" world.

Reality—truth—is that there is a God in heaven. Reality is that He made us and we are accountable to Him. Reality is that this God has spoken and what He says matters—eternally. Reality is that without His salvation, we are doomed to eternal torment. Reality is that God's Son, Jesus Christ, has died for the sins of the world, that He has risen again, and that whoever believes on Him is given eternal life.

This is the *real world*, and only a believer walking in fellowship with His Creator and Redeemer can understand it. Everyone else in the world is experiencing a "break with reality." No wonder those who do not know Christ—and believers who are ignoring God's Word— live and act as if they have gone mad. The only world they *can* know doesn't make sense. *The reality of life is that life isn't supposed to make sense or bring any lasting peace and satisfaction without God.*

An Alien in Times Square

To illustrate the emotional turmoil we can expect in our society when the majority of its citizens do not understand the *real* world (as God has made it and reveals it to us), imagine that you know a missionary who works with tribes in the Amazon interior of South America. These tribesmen have never seen an outsider and do not understand the language or the ways of the outside world.

Suppose this missionary were to bring one of these nationals out of the heart of the Amazon rain forest and abandon him, untaught and alone, in Times Square in New York City. It would be obvious that this poor Amazonian does not know how to get along in Times Square. He will have experiences that are entirely outside his frame of reference. While he tries to survive and find food and shelter, he will experience many upsetting events.

Think for a moment about what his emotions and behaviors might be during the first several days of his visit to this strange new situation. He will obviously be *fearful* because he does not understand what is going on around him. He will no doubt eventually feel *angry* because he is constantly *frustrated*. Nothing he attempts to do will work as it did back in his homeland. He will be filled with *confusion*. He will perhaps be *depressed* as he considers giving up, but where will he go to quit? He may become *violent* out of *desperation*. Times Square will present him with a reality he does not understand and therefore cannot function in effectively.

The result is a man who will soon show many of the "emotional disorders" we see in today's society in general. While the Amazonian tribesman is out of touch with his newfound reality in New York City, most of the rest of those in Times Square are just as out of touch with a much greater reality—God—and are experiencing the same emotional struggles and destructive behaviors, but for a different reason.[8]

You see, *God* is the environment of man. Paul says, "For in [God] we live, and move, and have our being" (Acts 17:28). The Amazonian cannot solve his New York problems his *own way*. By the same token, man's *own way* will not work in God's world, and one who attempts to live independent of the knowledge and ways of God will experience a "break with reality." Our despondency, anger, worry, fear, guilt, bitterness, lust, and so forth are indications that the dependent love *relationship* with God has grown cold—or has never been developed in the first place. These problems show us we are "out of teach" with reality.

God tells the prophet Jeremiah that His people have committed two evils. The first evil is that they have forsaken God, who is the fountain of living waters. He is the only source of spiritual refreshment and life. The second evil is that they then sought to quench their thirst by digging cisterns—holes dug into the ground to catch runoff water from the roof. Those cisterns, however, were damaged. They couldn't hold the water.

We do the same thing. We easily forsake fellowship with God as the source of our refreshment and life and turn to some other means to satisfy our lives. God says this is a great evil.

1. Memorize Jeremiah 2:13 (Memory Card 32).

For my people have committed two evils; they have forsaken me the fountain of living waters, and hewed them out cisterns, broken cisterns, that can hold no water.

---

[8] The illustration of the Amazonian is an expanded adaptation of a similar illustration in *Knowing God* by J. I. Packer (Downers Grove, Ill.: InterVarsity Press, 1973), 14-15.

Hello! Anybody There?

Most of us have experienced a lost connection between our telephone and that of a friend we were talking to. We re-dialed the number and the connection was restored. Fellowship with God is blocked by the sin of going our *own way* in some aspect of life. The connection is restored upon our repentance. Once restored to fellowship with God, we have the opportunity to develop a dependent, personal relationship with God. Unfortunately, once the connection is restored with God, many people do not know what to say to the Person "on the other end of the line." They do not know how to develop a relationship with God. We will explore the dynamics of what needs to be happening between God and us in this unit.

2. Considering the telephone analogy above, check below the statement that best represents your relationship with God.

   ☐ I am so distant from God that I feel as if there is no real connection with Him at all.

   ☐ I know that God tries to speak to me, but I feel as if there is a great deal of static on the line. I'm not very good at listening to what He says, and I rarely have any significant conversation with Him.

   ☐ I have some times of wonderful fellowship and conversation with God. I feel at times that I really make headway in my personal relationship with Him, but I must confess that those times are much farther apart than they should be.

   ☐ I stay in pretty close communication with God. I'm fairly sensitive to Him when He speaks to me from His Word, and I talk with Him formally and informally many times a day.

3. **Memorize John 15:4-5 (Memory Card 33).**

   Abide in me, and I in you. As the branch cannot bear fruit of itself, except it abide in the vine; no more can ye, except ye abide in me. I am the vine, ye are the branches: He that abideth in me, and I in him, the same bringeth forth much fruit: for without me ye can do nothing.

4. Memorize Psalm 42:1-2 (Memory Card 34).

> *As the hart[9] panteth after the water brooks, so panteth my soul after thee, O God. My soul thirsteth for God, for the living God.*

To complete this checkpoint, you must read all the text, fill in the blank and memorize Jeremiah 2:13, John 15:4-5, and Psalm 42:1-2.

☐ Text read.............................Date completed: _____ Initials: _____

☐ Blanks filled in ....Date completed: _____ Initials: _____

☐ Jeremiah 2:13 ....Date completed: _____ Initials: _____

☐ John 15:4-5.............................Date completed: _____ Initials: _____

☐ Psalm 42:1-2.............................Date completed: _____ Initials: _____

I have completed Checkpoint 1.

Your name	Date
Group Leader's name	Date

CHECKPOINT 2 – MORE THAN BEING ON SPEAKING TERMS

Man was made to function well only when in fellowship with His Creator. Fellowship, in the way we are speaking about it, means more than just having all known sin confessed. Your care group leader may ask you, "Are you in fellowship with God at this moment, or is there a barrier between you and God?"

Having all known sin confessed is a crucial starting point (1 John 1:9), but it is just that—a starting point. Fellowship with God is possible when there is "nothing between my soul and the Savior," as the hymn writer put it; but there must also be much *going on* between my soul and the Savior.

---

[9] Hart is an Old English word for a deer.

Any person who has read the Bible very much is aware that certain Bible characters seem to stand above their peers in the quality of their relationship with God. For example, Abraham was called "the Friend of God" (James 2:23). Moses spoke with God "face to face, as a man speaketh unto his friend" (Exodus 33:11). Genesis 5:24 tells us that "Enoch walked with God." God Himself called David "a man after his own heart" (1 Samuel 13:14). Their relationships with God were not unique experiences that no one else can have. *Any one of us can have that kind of relationship with God.* Let's look at how it can be our experience too.

Something Is Going on Between Them!

One of the blessings of working in a college environment is seeing God drawing together couples who eventually marry. In class a professor will often notice a couple sitting together but will not think anything about it until he sees them consistently walking to and from the class together. As he watches them before class begins, he will notice that they talk to each other in low tones, almost oblivious to the people around them. There is an obvious admiration for each other in their faces. While they may comment to each other about various events around them, most of their conversation is about each other. They discover something else about the other person and then comment on and compliment what they see in that person. They explore each other's opinions, likes, dislikes, family backgrounds, interests, and knowledge about various topics.

They seem never to have enough time to be with each other, and they plan times when they can see each other again. At first, each may pursue the relationship because of the delight each one receives from the other. If godly love is central in the relationship, however, each will become increasingly motivated to be a delight to the other.

If they truly delight in each other, they will not be able to keep their joy a secret. They will praise their friend to roommates, family, and anyone else who will listen. In fact, anyone who has much contact with either of them will see there is something going on between them. Relationships like this are characterized by *continual personal interaction*.

A relationship with God includes the same basic elements of learning *about* Him, followed by much personal interaction *with* Him. Knowing God in a personal way requires two initial elements, which we will look at in the next two checkpoints.

You may not have thought about it very much, but God wants to have this kind of loving relationship with each of His children. Our sin was the barrier that kept us from enjoying His fellowship, but He loved us enough to send His Son, Jesus, to die in our place in order to remove the barrier.

1. **Memorize 1 John 4:9-10 (Memory Card 35).**

   In this was manifest the love of God toward us, because that God sent his only begotten Son into the world, that we might live through him. Herein is love, not that we loved God, but that he loved us, and sent his Son to be the propitiation for our sins.

   NOTE: Let me explain the word *propitiation* in the verses above. All of the human race apart from Christ is already sentenced to experience the just wrath of God in hell along with Satan. The sacrifice of Jesus Christ on our behalf *satisfied*—or propitiated—the justice and wrath of God. This allowed Him to bring us into the family as His children and bless us through His Son, Jesus.

2. **Memorize 1 John 3:1-3 (Memory Card 36).**

   Behold, what manner of love the Father hath bestowed upon us, that we should be called the sons of God: therefore the world knoweth us not, because it knew him not. Beloved, now are we the sons of God, and it doth not yet appear what we shall be: but we know that when he shall appear, we shall be like him; for we shall see him as he is. And every man that hath this hope in him purifieth himself, even as he is pure.

To complete this checkpoint, you must read all the text, fill in the blanks, and memorize 1 John 4:9-10 and 1 John 3:1-3.

☐ Text read.........................Date completed: _____ Initials: _____

☐ Blanks filled in ....Date completed: _____ Initials: _____

☐ 1 John 4:9-10 ....Date completed: _____   Initials: _____

☐ 1 John 3:1-3...............................Date completed: _____   Initials: _____

I have completed Checkpoint 2.

_____	_____
Your name	Date
_____	_____
Group Leader's name	Date

CHECKPOINT 3 – KNOWING GOD REQUIRES THAT WE HAVE A DESIRE FOR HIM

Our greatest need is for God, yet because of our sinful bent (which is still a part of us, even after salvation), we often resort to going our *own way*. That path leads us directly away from God. God reminds us that the way that "seemeth right unto a man" leads to "death" (Proverbs 14:12).

Fortunately, *God places within those of us who are His children a desire for a relationship with Him.* This is not something we work up ourselves; it is the work of God. Philippians 2:13 says, "For it is God which worketh in you both to will and to do of his good pleasure." He is at work in every believer creating a "will" and an ability "to do" what is "His good pleasure." In Jeremiah 31:3 God speaks of His initiative in drawing men to Himself.

1. **Memorize Jeremiah 31:3 (Memory Card 37).**

   The Lord hath appeared of old unto me, saying, Yea, I have loved thee with an everlasting love: therefore with lovingkindness have I drawn thee.

Did you notice that last phrase? God says that *He* has drawn us to Himself. He initiated the relationship with us. He wants to have fellowship with us.

In Revelation 3:20 Christ is portrayed as standing outside the door of the believer's heart knocking. It is clear that Christ, not the believer, is taking the initiative for the relationship. Just as God sought Adam and Even in the Garden of Eden in order to continue fellowship with them (Genesis 3:8-9), so God continues to seek us so that we can have a personal, trusting relationship with Him. In his account of the battle between his flesh and his spirit, Paul said, "I know that in me (that is, in my flesh,) dwelleth no good thing: for *to will is present with me*" (Romans 7:18). He is testifying that within him is a continual desire ("will") to do right. That is the work of the Spirit of God and is an evidence of salvation.

God has created in man the desire for Him and has offered Himself as the object of man's desire! He is the only One sufficient to fill the God-shaped hole within man's soul. Augustine in his *Confessions* writes, "Thou madest us for Thyself, and our heart is restless, until it repose [finds its rest] in Thee." Notice the psalmist's desire for God in these next verses, which you will be memorizing.

2. Memorize Psalm 63:1 (Memory Card 38).

O God, thou art my God; early will I seek thee: my soul thirsteth for thee, my flesh longeth for thee in a dry and thirsty land, where no water is.

3. Memorize Psalm 73:25-26 (Memory Card 39).

Whom have I in heaven but thee? and there is none upon earth that I desire beside thee. My flesh and my heart faileth: but God is the strength of my heart, and my portion for ever.

4. Memorize Psalm 84:2 (Memory Card 40).

My soul longeth, yea, even fainteth for the courts of the Lord: my heart and my flesh crieth out for the living God.

God is glorified when man takes his place of joyful, grateful dependence because then God is exalted to His place as the only worthy, all-sufficient object of that dependence. David testifies of it this way:

"Their sorrows shall be multiplied that hasten after another god: . . . [but] I have set the Lord always before me: because he is at my right hand, I shall not be moved. Therefore my heart is glad, and my glory rejoiceth: my [soul] also shall rest in hope. . . . Thou wilt show me the path of life: in thy presence is fulness of joy; at thy right hand there are pleasures for evermore" (Psalm 16:4, 8-9, 11).

Make no mistake about it. If you are God's child, He has placed within you a desire for Himself. *If your only desires in life are for yourself and for relief from your problems, and you experience no desire whatsoever for a relationship with God, your first step needs to be a very careful examination of whether or not you even belong to Him.* Those who are truly members of His family experience a God-given desire for intimacy with their Father.

If you are a child of God and have been using drugs, alcohol, or dealing with some major trauma in your life, your desire for God may be pushed to the back of your heart. If you are a true believer and take some time to think honestly about your heart,along with your desire to have deliverance from whatever problems seem to plague your life, you will have a desire for a better relationship with God. In fact, you may feel frustrated that the kind of relationship with Him that you desire seems so elusive. An unbeliever never experiences this kind of frustration. *An unbeliever may know he does not have fellowship with God, but it does not bother him.* He is content to see his own solutions to his own problems—apart from God.

The desire for God is, first, an assurance that we are His children. It is, second, a sign that He is at work in our lives, since a desire for God cannot be generated on our own. A desire for God also shows that He is intending to do more in us for our good and for His ultimate glory. Jesus said in the Beatitudes, "Blessed are they which do hunger and thirst after righteousness: *for they shall be filled*" (Matthew 5:6).

Knowing God requires that we have a desire for Him. He places that desire within us if we are His child. Knowing God requires something else, however, that we will look at in the next checkpoint.

5. Strong personal relationships are characterized by frequent personal interaction. Discuss specific things that will have to change with your relationship to God before you can say you have frequent personal interaction. If your relationship with God is already at this level, describe the kind of frequent personal interactions that you enjoy with Him.

_____

_____

_____

_____

_____

_____

_____

_____

☐ Text read........................Date completed: _____ Initials: _____

☐ Blanks filled in ....Date completed: _____ Initials: _____

☐ Jeremiah 31:3 ....Date completed: _____ Initials: _____

☐ Psalm 63:1......................Date completed: _____ Initials: _____

☐ Psalm 73:25-26..............Date completed: _____ Initials: _____

☐ Psalm 84:2......................Date completed: _____ Initials: _____

I have completed Checkpoint 3.

_____   _____
Your name   Date

_____   _____
Group Leader's name   Date

CHECKPOINT 4 – KNOWING GOD REQUIRES THAT WE SEEK GOD WHOLEHEARTEDLY

God promises that those who respond to the desire He places within them by seeking Him will not be disappointed.

1. **Memorize Deuteronomy 4:29 (Memory Card 41).**

   But if from thence thou shalt seek the Lord thy God, thou shalt find him, if thou seek him with all thy heart and with all thy soul.

Deuteronomy 4:29, quoted above, says that we must seek God *with all our heart.* A common complaint about modern Christians is that they are apathetic. That is not entirely true. They are very passionate people. By passionate, I do not mean necessarily that they are sensual. I mean instead that they are *wholehearted* about something. Notice their passion for sports, entertainment, leisure, adventure, fashions, sex, wealth, or achievement. Everyone is passionate! He either loves himself (thus the passion for those things that please himself), or he loves God and his neighbor. *Apathy toward God is the result of being passionate about something else you want more.* Jesus was quite clear on this issue.

2. **Memorize Matthew 6:24 (Memory Card 42).**

   No man can serve two masters: for either he will hate the one, and love the other; or else he will hold to the one, and despise the other. Ye cannot serve God and mammon.[10]

Note that He said that while man despises (considers small) and hates one thing, he *loves* the other thing. If he considers God and His interests a small thing, it is because he is passionate about something else.

Jesus rebuked Peter one time because Peter was valuing the things of the world more than the things of Jesus' kingdom. In Matthew 16:23-25 Jesus addressed Peter's misdirected passion.

   But [Jesus] turned, and said unto Peter, Get thee behind me, Satan: thou art an offence unto me: for thou savourest not the

---

[10]*Mammon* is an Old English word for money or possessions.

things that be of God, but those that be of men. Then said Jesus unto his disciples, If any man will come after me, let him deny himself, and take up his cross, and follow me. For whosoever will save his life shall lose it: and whosoever will lose his life for my sake shall find it.

Jesus said in the Beatitudes that only the "pure in heart" could "see God" (Matthew 5:8). "Pure in heart" does not mean the absence of sin, although that is certainly a part of the meaning. It means to have a single, undivided heart. It is free (pure) from other conflicting priorities. God takes double-mindedness very seriously. He compares Himself to a spouse with an unfaithful partner and compares the believer whose first love is not for Christ to the spouse having an illicit sexual affair.

3. Memorize James 4:4, 8, 10 (Memory Card 43).

Ye adulterers and adulteresses, know ye not that the friendship of the world is enmity with God? whosoever therefore will be a friend of the world is the enemy of God . . . Draw nigh to God, and he will draw night to you. Cleanse your hands, ye sinners; and purify your hearts, ye double minded. . . Humble yourselves in the sight of the Lord, and he shall lift you up.

We can have a personal, dependent relationship with God if we are willing to seek Him and forsake all other loves. No young lady is going to be impressed by a young man proposing marriage if he insists on continuing to date other girls. If the marriage relationship is to be lasting and meaningful, each must love the other exclusively and wholeheartedly. Similarly, as Creator and Sustainer of all, God deserves first place in our lives—and demands it—if we are to know Him in any kind of personal, intimate way.

Please understand that the information in this unit is not incidental to, but is the heart of, biblical change. *Any attempts to solve the problems of life apart from a dependent relationship with God are both arrogant and, in the long run, ineffective.*

4. Do you strongly agree, somewhat agree, mildly disagree, or strongly disagree with the above sentence in italics? _____ Explain your answer.

_____

_____

_____

_____

5. The text says, *"Apathy toward God is the result of being passionate about something else you want more."* What desires in your life tend to overshadow and quench your desire for a relationship with God.

_____

_____

_____

_____

To complete this checkpoint, you must read all the text, fill in the blanks, and memorize Deuteronomy 4:29, Matthew 6:24, and James 4:4, 8, 10.

☐ Text read.............................Date completed: _____ Initials: _____

☐ Blanks filled in ....Date completed: _____ Initials: _____

☐ Deuteronomy 4:29...................Date completed: _____ Initials: _____

☐ Matthew 6:24............................Date completed: _____ Initials: _____

☐ James 4:4, 8, 10.........................Date completed: _____ Initials: _____

I have completed Checkpoint 4.

_____   _____
Your name   Date

_____   _____
Group Leader's name   Date

CHECKPOINT 5 – KNOWING GOD REQUIRES THAT WE SEEK HIM PERSONALLY

Seeking God is not just an exercise in exploring Bible content or studying theology. Those pursuits play an important part in knowing God, but they are only means to an end—never ends in themselves. The following dialogue illustrates the proper approach when seeking to know God.

A Conversation with Coach

Phil played first string on the soccer team for his Christian high school. One day after soccer practice, Phil jogged over to the bleachers and sat down on the bench next to his coach. They exchanged greetings and talked briefly about the scrimmage the team had just finished. Finally, Phil posed a question.

"Coach, I've been struggling with something in my spiritual life recently and wonder if I could talk to you about it."

"Sure, Phil, what's up?"

"Well, since my decision at summer teen camp to live for the Lord, I have really made an effort to be faithful in reading my Bible and spending some time in prayer every day. It hasn't been easy, but I've been pretty faithful."

"If it's any encouragement to you, Phil, the difference in you this year is noticeable. You used to be far more uptight about things that didn't go your way. I have really been encouraged."

"Thanks, Coach, but I really feel that something is still missing. In addition to my regular devotions, I volunteered to lead singing when the youth group does the Wednesday night service at the rescue mission, and I started the Thursday morning prayer meeting for the seniors before first-hour class at school. But even with all these things going on, I still feel as if my heart is so cold toward God. I'm doing a lot of the right things now, and I really am glad I'm doing them, but there has to be something more to the Christian life."

"Phil, let me ask you a question about the time you spend reading your Bible each day. When you open your Bible to read every day, what are you looking for?"

"Well, I have been reading through the New Testament, and I usually try to find something that will encourage me for the day or a principle I can apply."

"That's fine, Phil, but do you have any idea why God gave us the Bible in the first place?"

"I guess He gave it as a guidebook for life?"

"It certainly does teach us how to live, Phil, but it is far more than that. When you get home, look up 1 John 5:9. It says, "'This is the witness of *God,* which he hath testified of his *Son.*' There is a *Person* at the center of everything you read in the Bible. If you merely look for the principles and encouraging passages, you will find what you are looking for, but you will miss God in the process."

"I've never thought of it that way before, Coach."

"Let me give you an example. Since you have been reading in the New Testament, you have probably read the account in John 6 of Jesus feeding the five thousand."

"Yes, I read that sometime last week. I'm almost through the four Gospels now."

"God did not put that account in the Bible as an explanation of how we ought to feed large numbers of people when we have a church picnic. It was given to reveal something to us about God's Son, Jesus Christ. You have to stop and ask yourself, 'What does this passage reveal about Jesus Christ?' In fact, you may want to make yourself a bookmark for your Bible with that question on it. You have to look for a *Person* in the Scriptures if you are to have a *personal* relationship with God. When it becomes just a source of principles to you, then you will find your heart cold. This account in John shows us His great compassion for people in need and His great ability to meet that need. It also shows us that He purposefully arranges situations to test the faith of His disciples.

"His compassion and power are two of His attributes. You might stop right there and ask yourself further, 'What is compassion? What else do I know about God's compassion? Who else in the Bible experienced it? Who else in the Bible demonstrated it? How has God personally demonstrated compassion to me? Since I am called to be Christlike, how am I doing at displaying compassion? If it has been lacking in my daily contacts with people, what have others been seeing in me instead of the compassion that would been Christlike in those situations?'"

"You might spend thirty or forty minutes on this one attribute, taking notes, praying for God to 'search' you and 'try' you as David prayed in Psalm 139:23 and thanking Him for showing you more about Himself. You might make a list of people that you tend to shun—maybe here at school, maybe in your youth group, or maybe at the rescue mission. You might jot a note after each name, spelling out what you could do to make a difference in each life by showing compassion in some way as Jude 22 teaches. You could then spend time praying for them that God would use you as a channel of His love to them to draw them into a more personal relationship with God as well. You would want to thank God for showing you more of Himself, and you would want to express to Him that it is this kind of excellence in Him that makes you glad that you are His child. You could tell Him about the delight that these verses have been to you as you have meditated upon them. You might even want to write out a special prayer of thanksgiving in a journal to remind you of what you have told Him."

"Wow, Coach! I never thought of my daily devotions like that before; that's pretty exciting! I can see how it makes everything more personal, and it would certainly change me more."

"Phil, what I have just described to you is what the Bible calls meditation. It is not merely studying the Bible to learn more principles, although they are important. It is studying the Bible to learn more about a *Person*—God Himself. The principles you find along the way are manifestations of His character. If you don't see the Person behind the principles, you have missed God's intention for His revelation. Of course, you probably can't take an hour every day for this kind of study, but you should consider setting aside a significant block of time on the weekend that you will spend seeking the Lord in this way. It won't be long before you are looking for ways to spend more time like this with Him throughout the week in addition to your daily Bible reading and prayer. Your daily devotional time becomes an extension of the larger chunks of time you are spending with God on the weekend. Thank about the words of William Longstaff's hymn, 'Take Time to Be Holy.' The second stanza says,

> *Take time to be holy; the world rushes on.*
> *Spend much time in secret with Jesus alone.*
> *By looking to Jesus, like Him thou shalt be.*
> *Thy friends in thy conduct, His likeness shall see.*

You really can't find lasting joy or peace any other way. You have to take the Bible *personally* and treat God like a *Person* before your heart will be warmed."

"Thanks, Coach! You've given me a lot to think about. I'll change my approach and let you know in a few days how things are going."

Phil's coach is right. He described to Phil a relationship with God based upon *fellowship—personal interactions with God.* This kind of interaction with God delights Him because we are finding our delight in Him.

1. What practical lessons for your own relationship with God did you learn from Phil's conversation with his coach?

_____

_____

_____

_____

_____

_____

In Psalm 1, David speaks of the kind of relationship with God that meditates upon His Word and produces delight and stability in the believer.

2. Memorize Psalm 1:1-2 (Memory Card 44).

Blessed is the man that walketh not in the counsel of the ungodly, nor standeth in the way of sinners, nor sitteth in the seat of the scornful. But his delight is in the law of the Lord: and in his law doth he meditate day and night.

3. Memorize Psalm 1:3 (Memory Card 45).

And he shall be like a tree planted by the rivers of water, that bringeth forth his fruit in his season: his leaf also shall not wither; and whatsoever he doeth shall prosper.

4. Memorize Psalm 1:4-5 (Memory Card 46).

The ungodly are not so: but are like the chaff which the wind driveth away. Therefore the ungodly shall not stand in the judgment, nor sinners in the congregation of the righteous.

To complete this checkpoint, you must read all the text, fill in the blanks, memorize Psalm 1:1-2, 3, and 4-5.

☐ Text read.........................Date completed: _____ Initials: _____

☐ Blanks filled in ....Date completed: _____ Initials: _____

☐ Psalm 1:1-2 ....Date completed: _____ Initials: _____

☐ Psalm 1:3 ....Date completed: _____ Initials: _____

☐ Psalm 1:4-5 ....Date completed: _____ Initials: _____

I have completed Checkpoint 5.

_____   _____
Your name   Date

_____   _____
Group Leader's name   Date

CHECKPOINT 6 – JOURNAL WORK

To complete this checkpoint you must journal ten days in a row.

I have completed Checkpoint 6.

_____   _____
Your name   Date

_____   _____
Group Leader's name   Date

CHECKPOINT 7 – CHURCH ATTENDANCE

To complete this checkpoint, you must do the following:

1. Attend two or more church services within one week. They can be the Sunday morning worship service, a Sunday school class, a Sunday evening service, or a midweek service (sometimes called "prayer meeting").

2. Fill in the information below, and have a pastor of the church sign the proper blank below.

Name of the church: _____

Check the services you attended:

☐ Sunday school

☐ Sunday morning worship service

☐ Sunday evening service

☐ Midweek service

☐ Other (explain): _____

Pastor's signature: _____

I have completed Checkpoint 7.

Your name	Date
Group Leader's name	Date

CHECKPOINT 8 – WRITTEN REPORT ON "KNOWING GOD"

To complete this checkpoint, write a one-page paper explaining the important truths you have learned in this lesson. To write the paper you will need to review your answers to remind yourself of what you have learned. Grammar and spelling are not an issue. Do the best you can, asking God to help you understand the importance of learning the process of how we grow and change.

I have completed Checkpoint 8.

Your name	Date
Group Leader's name	Date

CHECKPOINT 9 — SERVICE OPPORTUNITY

An important part of Christian living is serving God and others. To complete this checkpoint, you must go with a group leader, *Freedom That Lasts* director, pastor, or other mature person your pastor or director assigns to visit new students who have attended *Freedom That Lasts*.

Write out in the blanks below whom you went with and whom you visited and summarize how the visits turned out.

_____

_____

_____

_____

_____

_____

_____

_____

_____

_____

_____

_____

_____

_____

_____

_____

_____

_____

_____

I have completed Checkpoint 9.

_____   _____
Your name   Date

_____   _____
Group Leader's name   Date

CONGRATULATIONS!

You have completed the nine checkpoints necessary to finish this unit. The road map towards growth and change into Christlikeness should be clearer to you now.

When you finish all the checkpoints for this unit and your group leader has signed off on them, you will receive your reward at the end of that class. We encourage you to invite your friends and family to witness your accomplishment.

If you will continue the lessons in this book and faithfully use your *Spiritual Life Journal,* you will come to know your God much, much better than you do now!

UNIT 6

CHRISTLIKENESS

> But we all with [unobstructed view] beholding as in a [a mirror] the glory of the Lord, are changed into the same image from glory to glory, even as by the Spirit of the Lord.
> (2 Corinthians 3:18)

CHECKPOINT 1 – CHANGED BY HIS GLORY

Our study in this unit will begin to explore the specific process whereby we are changed by the Spirit of God into the image of Christ. We saw in the last unit that God must draw a man to Himself and that the man must respond with a wholehearted pursuit of God. God must be treated personally; then He will respond personally to the searching believer. If you have asked God to forgive any known sin in your heart and have forsaken any personal desires to quench your desire for God, you are ready to make some exciting steps spiritually as God shows you Himself in His Word.

1. **Memorize 2 Corinthians 3:18 (Memory Card 47).**

   But we all, with open face beholding as in a glass the glory of the Lord, are changed into the same image from glory to glory, even as by the Spirit of the Lord.

Second Corinthians 3:18 teaches us that as God shows us His glory in the Word, we experience a very specific change. By God's Spirit, we display an ever-increasing reflection of those "glories" in our own lives. We need to ask ourselves then, "What is God's glory?"

God's glory is the manifestation of His many-splendored excellencies. It was shown in the Old Testament as a Shekinah—a radiant reflection of God's nature too brilliant for any human to view directly. It was the overwhelming presence of His perfection.

When we look at the sun, we see its white light—all of its colors mixed together. If we look at sunlight through a prism, we see the white light broken up into its individual colors of the rainbow. A few men saw the "white light" of God's glory. They were almost blinded by the manifestation, as if looking at the sun directly, and fell on their faces in stunned humility. Read the passages below to see these testimonies of the glory of God.

2. Read Exodus 24:12-18.

    ☐ Check the box when you have read the passage.

3. Read Ezekiel 1:26-28.

    ☐ Check the box when you have read the passage.

4. Read Revelation 1:12-18.

    ☐ Check the box when you have read the passage.

Most people in the Scriptures who saw God, however, did not see this kind of blinding vision of the Lord. Rather than the "white light" of His glory, they saw the individual "colors"—individual attributes or characteristics of God. God revealed some aspect of Himself by giving people one of His names, which stand for some part of His character. Sometimes the way He dealt with the nation Israel or with an individual was to show some characteristic of Himself—perhaps His faithfulness, His compassion, His power, His mercy, His covenant love, and so forth. His law given to Moses revealed the holiness of His nature. The behavioral codes of the Pentateuch showed aspects of His righteousness and His wisdom.[11]

In the New Testament, God's specific "glories" or attributes were demonstrated more clearly in the earthly life of Jesus Christ. The apostle John spoke of that in John 1:14.

5. Memorize John 1:14 (Memory Card 48).

> *And the Word was made flesh, and dwelt among us, (and we beheld his glory, the glory as of the only begotten of the Father,) full of grace and truth.*

Second Corinthians 3:18 tells us that we can be changed as we are exposed to the "glories"—these attributes of God as they are revealed to us by God's Spirit through the Scriptures. Let's take a closer look at God's attributes.

More About God's Attributes

Some theologians divide the attributes of God into *communicable* and *noncommunicable* attributes. We use these two terms more commonly to talk about diseases. A communicable disease, like measles, is one you can "get" from someone else. A noncommunicable disease, like cancer, is one that cannot be passed from one person to another through normal contact. Likewise, a noncommunicable attribute is one that no creature of God can "get." Some of God's noncommunicable attributes are the following:

Omnipotence—God is all powerful.

Omniscience—God knows everything.

Omnipresence—God is everywhere at all times.

Immutability—God's nature never changes.

Transcendence—God is distinctly different from His creation.

Eternality—God has no beginning or end.

---

[11]The Pentateuch is a word for the first five books of the Old Testament, all of which were written by Moses. The Pentateuch contains Genesis, Exodus, Leviticus, Numbers, and Deuteronomy.

Being like Christ does not involve acquiring any of these attributes. That is impossible. *Being Christlike, however, means acquiring His communicable attributes.*

6. God gives us several lists of Christlike qualities. *You have studied the most important ones in Student Manual 1 when you studied the virtues of 2 Peter 1:5-7.* List those virtues below and then list the additional virtues found in Galatians 5:22-23, Matthew 5:1-12, 1 Corinthians 13:4-8, and James 3:17-18. These are all communicable attributes of God—those He wants us to "get" in the sanctification process.

_____

_____

_____

_____

_____

_____

_____

_____

_____

_____

_____

_____

_____

These are all communicable attributes of God. That means that God possesses these qualities and that any believer can "get" them as he obeys God's Word with God's help. When Jesus walked on this earth, these were characteristics of His life. These are what come out of the "tea bag" of a Spirit-filled believer when he is put into "hot water" situations. When he manifests these characteristics on a consistent basis even under pressure, we say he has Christian (Christlike) character.

To complete this checkpoint, you must read all the text, fill in the blanks, and memorize 2 Corinthians 3:18 and John 1:14.

☐ Text read..Date completed: _____ Initials: _____

☐ Blanks filled in ....Date completed: _____ Initials: _____

☐ 2 Corinthians 3:18.....................Date completed: _____ Initials: _____

☐ John 1:14.......................................Date completed: _____ Initials: _____

I have completed Checkpoint 1.

_____   _____
Your name   Date

_____   _____
Group Leader's name   Date

CHECKPOINT 2 – ILLUMINATION: WHEN GOD TURNS THE LIGHT ON

Let's look at the actual process of change more closely. *We must not think that the Bible alone changes a man.* God's Spirit must personally show the realities of God to that man as he ponders the Scriptures. This divine work is called "illumination."

In Matthew 16:13 Jesus asked His disciples, "Whom do men say that I the Son of man am?" They replied that some thought He was John the Baptist and that others thought He was one of the prophets— perhaps Elijah or Jeremiah. He asked them a more pointed question in verse 15: "But whom say *ye* that I am? Peter answered with a powerful statement of reality in verse 16.

1. Look up Matthew 16:16 and write it out below.

_____

_____

_____

Jesus' reply to Peter is instructive to us at this point in our study. Our Lord said, "Blessed art thou, Simon Bar-jona: *for flesh and blood hath not revealed it unto thee, but my Father which is in heaven*" (v. 17).

Jesus said in effect, "Peter, you have experienced something that is not common to all men. You cannot learn what you have learned by natural means. My Father Himself showed you this truth. He opened your eyes and you were illuminated." Let me illustrate it this way.

Tanned by the Sun

Most fair-skinned people exposed to the sun for an extended period of time working in their garden or yard must shield themselves from the sun to avoid serious sunburn. Direct exposure to the sun will have an automatic effect on their skin. Tanning is not something they do to themselves. If the tan is a "vacation tan"—one they got while on a vacation where they spent more time in the sun—it will gradually disappear when they return to their normal routine out of the sun.

Likewise, change into Christlikeness is not something we do *to* ourselves. *It happens supernaturally through the working of the Holy Spirit when we expose ourselves to God's Word and He reveals His glory, and with His help, we imitate His character.*

A fair-skinned man who is not tanned as much as he would like can do only one thing—spend more time in the sun.[12] In fact, if a dark tan is truly important to him, he will not be watching the clock to see whether his "fifteen minutes" of time in the sun is up; he will be watching his skin to see whether it has the color he wants. If he wants a darker tan than his time in the sun gave him today, he will look

---

[12] Please do not consider this illustration an endorsement of some people's fascination with tanning. Tanning can be fraught with all sorts of medical problems (e.g., cancer) and raises questionable issues (e.g., partial nudity). The effect of the sun on human skin, however, has some direct parallels to the effect of the glory of God on the believer's soul.

at what he has to do tomorrow to see whether he can postpone or eliminate anything in order to spend more time in the sun.

In the same way, a believer who is not manifesting the character of Jesus in some area of his life can do only one thing—*spend more time in the Word asking God to illuminate his mind and heart.* Believers who have very little "tan" are revealing their limited exposure to the glory of God. If we aren't spending time "walking in the light," our "untanned" (unchanged) lives show that our walk has been mostly "in darkness." If we truly want more change in our lives, we will look at what is on our agenda today to see whether anything can be postponed or eliminated so that we can spend more time being exposed to the glory of God. We won't be watching the clock; we will be watching for the effect of the glory of God on our lives.

Youth directors and pastors are aware of a phenomenon common to young people who go to a summer Bible camp and make decisions for the Lord. The decisions to give up their ungodly friends, bad habits, worldly music, and so forth seem to last for only a couple of weeks. The teen's desire and resolve seem to weaken over time. He eventually returns to his former lifestyle pretty discouraged and perhaps even cynical because he loses hope that change is possible for him. Onlookers note the slide back into his old ways and comment that he made just a "camp decision." Unfortunately, many adults come to expect this phenomenon—an attitude that betrays a shallow understanding of biblical change.

Suppose we were to take the same attitude toward a friend who came back from a vacation at the ocean three weeks ago. He came back very tanned because of the time he had spent in the sun, but now his tan is fading. We wouldn't say that his "vacation tan" wasn't real because it didn't last! We would all understand that unless he keeps up the same level of exposure to the sun that gave him the tan in the first place, he will not keep the tan.

Likewise, we must understand that any decisions we make for the Lord because of time we have spent with Him can be maintained only by generous amounts of exposure to God's Word and by prayer that the Lord will continue His work of illumination in our heart. Notice the emphasis in the verses below upon "continuing" in the Word for its full effect.

2. **Memorize James 1:22-23 (Memory Card 49).**

   But be ye doers of the word, and not hearers only, deceiving your own selves. For if any be a hearer of the word, and not a doer, he is like unto a man beholding his natural face in a glass.

3. **Memorize James 1:24-25 (Memory Card 50).**

   For he beholdeth himself, and goeth his way, and straightway forgetteth what manner of man he was. But whoso looketh into the perfect law of liberty, and continueth therein, he being not a forgetful hearer, but a doer of the work, this man shall be blessed in his deed.

4. What truth about God or about yourself has God shown you recently in His Word?

   _____

   _____

   _____

   _____

   _____

   _____

5. How will you make sure that the truths you listed above become a consistent part of your life? Be as specific as possible.

   _____

   _____

   _____

   _____

   _____

   _____

To complete this checkpoint, you must read all the text, fill in the blanks, and memorize James 1:22-23 and 1:24-25.

☐ Text read...................................Date completed: _____ Initials: _____

☐ Blanks filled in ....Date completed: _____ Initials: _____

☐ James 1:22-23...........................Date completed: _____ Initials: _____

☐ James 1:24-25...........................Date completed: _____ Initials: _____

I have completed Checkpoint 2.

_____   _____
Your name   Date

_____   _____
Group Leader's name   Date

CHECKPOINT 3 – EVIDENCES OF EXPOSURE TO GOD

All of us know the most obvious effect of time spent in the sun for a fair-skinned person—darker skin—but what happens when a man is exposed to the glory of God? What are the effects of illuminated truth upon the believer? Not all the effects we will discuss are present in the same proportion every time for every person who is illuminated, but there *will* be some effect. No man can see God or His truth and be unaffected by it. He will be moved in some way by the experience.

Illuminated Truth Brings Great Assurance to the Believer

Often when God's Spirit illuminates some Scripture passage, the believer sees afresh the *validity* of the truth. He is moved to have a steadfast confidence, an inner assurance. He says to himself, *"This is right; I must believe it!"*

An illuminated man is divinely persuaded that he has seen something from God and that what he has seen is right. He will boldly defy every assault of hell and will burn at the stake if necessary before he will deny the truth of what he has seen and knows to be true.

While the believer is intellectually convinced of the truth, he is also *humbled* by the experience. He is not cocky or arrogant in his knowledge. Every man in the Bible who truly saw some aspect of God and His nature was found "on his face." Whenever we see some area of our own life in contrast to God's nature, we will see our own great deficiency and rebellion in that area. We will be humbled and repentant.

In teen leadership camp, Chris and the rest of the teens were given an assignment to memorize and meditate upon Philippians 2:3-16 to learn about the servant nature of our Lord. They were challenged to look at how Christ denied Himself in order to be a servant to others. Jesus did not concern Himself about His reputation among His peers. He obeyed His Father to take the lowest form of created, rational beings—a man. He further obeyed His Father and submitted to His human authorities to the point of death, even death by a humiliating and excruciating form of Roman torture—crucifixion.

In a personal conference with one of the leadership speakers, Chris shared how God had humbled him as he spent several hours during the week meditating on the text and thinking of its ramifications for Christ and for himself. As part of the exercise, he was to list seventy-five ways he was selfish at home, at work, and at school. It was humbling enough to see how much he looked out for himself at the expense of others throughout his daily routine; it was painful for him to realize his own selfishness compared to the self-sacrifice of his Lord on his behalf. He sought the Lord's forgiveness and was ready for help on how to be more like Christ at home. He had been *humbled* when his illuminated heart saw one of the glories of the Lord—His humility.

The memory work for the rest of this unit will come from this very same passage. It is an important one that illustrates the Father's admiration for the humility of His Son demonstrated by His Son's obedience to His will. The Father wants to see this developed in us as well. Meditating upon Philippians 2:3-16 is a great place to start.

1. **Memorize Philippians 2:3-4 (Memory Card 51).**

   Let nothing be done through strife or vainglory; but in lowliness of mind let each esteem other better than themselves. Look not every man on his own things, but every man also on the things of others.

2. **Memorize Philippians 2:5-7 (Memory Card 52).**

   Let this mind be in you, which was also in Christ Jesus: who, being in the form of God, thought it not robbery to be equal with God: but made himself of no reputation, and took upon him the form of a servant, and was made in the likeness of men.

When we behold the glory of God and see some aspect of His nature, we are taught what that virtue truly looks like. In this illustration, Chris had thought he was a pretty good teen. In fact, if you were to ask his parents or his youth director at church what he was like, they would tell you that he was a model teen. He was leader of the church youth group and had a good testimony at home and at school. Without doubt Chris had been responsive to his earthly authorities and to God in the areas he knew about, but it was not until he had been exposed to some aspect of the glory of God that he learned what self-sacrificing love really looks like. When he saw it manifested in the Person and works of God's Son, he was shown a new, higher standard. When compared to the teens around him, Chris always came out on top. When he considered the self-sacrificing humility of God's Son, Chris realized how much further he had to go to be Christlike.

No man can be proud of his level of spiritual maturity or theological understanding when he has been exposed to God's nature. We "all have sinned, and *come short of the glory of God*" (Romans 3:23). He may have made some progress on his spiritual journey, but he will quickly be *taught* by the glory of God that he has many more miles to cover before he can say he has "arrived."

These are the impressions upon the mind of a Christian when he sees God. He is at the same time taught, humbled, and made bold. How can it be otherwise—he has seen God!

3. Jesus taught His disciples a similar lesson when He washed His disciple's feet. Peter thought he was doing pretty well until he

was exposed to this level of servant activity by his Master. After His actions, Jesus instructed them. Read the entire passage (John 13:1-17)

☐ Check the box when you have read the passage.

4. List the lessons Jesus was trying to teach His disciples in verses 12-17.

    _____

    _____

    _____

    _____

    _____

    _____

5. Complete this statement from this checkpoint's text.

    "An illuminated man is divinely _____
    that he has seen something from God and that what he has seen
    is _____."

6. Give an example of a time when God spoke to you from His Word and you knew the truth of what you saw because God opened the "eyes" of your heart to understand it.

    _____

    _____

    _____

    _____

    _____

    _____

To complete this checkpoint, you must read all the text, fill in the blanks, and memorize Philippians 2:3-4 and 2:5-7.

☐ Text read.....................................Date completed: _____ Initials: _____

☐ Blanks filled in ....Date completed: _____ Initials: _____

☐ Philippians 2:3-4.......................Date completed: _____ Initials: _____

☐ Philippians 2:5-7.......................Date completed: _____ Initials: _____

I have completed Checkpoint 3.

_____	_____
Your name	Date
_____	_____
Group Leader's name	Date

CHECKPOINT 4 – EVIDENCES OF EXPOSURE TO GOD, CONTINUED

Illuminated Truth Brings Great Satisfaction to the Believer

An illuminated believer viewing the glory of God also sees the *beauty* of the truth. He declares, *"This is wonderful; I must praise it!"*

The Word becomes attractive to him, and he finds himself admiring it. It may even be breath-taking. There is a new loveliness and worthiness about the truth to him. He cherishes it and delights in its splendor.

The result emotionally is twofold. First, there is great *joy* within him. Notice how David almost explodes with delight over the law of God in Psalm 119. The psalmist sees the glory of the Word, loves its taste, and praises its beauty. He sees the excellency of it. Peter called the effect, "unspeakable and full of glory" (1 Peter 1:8). An illuminated believer drinks deeply of this wellspring of joy, and others look with envy upon his continual feast of joy. Sometimes he is even overwhelmed by the hymns he sings. Their truth reminds him of what he has seen from God Himself. This joy is far more than the lightheartedness of a naturally exuberant, bubbling personality. It is the effect upon the soul of an illuminated man who has seen the glory of God.

Second, there is in him a great *peace*. Seeing God brings a great rest and steadiness to the soul. A man who is seeing truth illuminated by the Spirit of God is not agitated, restless, irritable, worried, or moody. He is at rest! He has seen God and that is enough. He is satisfied that nothing will separate him from the love of God and that God will use His power on his behalf as He wisely sees fit. Paul called it the "peace … which passeth all understanding" (Philippians 4:7).

Joy and peace blend together to show an effect in man greater than the sum of its two parts. The believer is *satisfied*. He is like a person who has just pushed his chair back from the Thanksgiving dinner table at his grandmother's home after stuffing himself with turkey, dressing, gravy, sweet potatoes, hot rolls, cranberry sauce, and pumpkin pie; he cannot be tempted with an invitation to eat a bologna sandwich. He is just too full to eat anything else. He is satisfied and content.

God made us to be completely satisfied with Himself. A believer who is beholding the glory of the Lord finds "fullness of joy" (Psalm 16:11). Such was the experience of the psalmist David. He was a "satisfied customer" because he had "tasted" and seen "that the Lord is good" (Psalm 34:8).

Many Christian organizations and churches are filled with discontented, frantic believers. Many of them are driven, perfectionistic, controlling people who never seem to be able to get everything checked off their lists. There is always something more to do. They never experience any real peace or rest because there is always something else out of control at the moment. If for some reason life quiets down for a few moments, they worry about what could go out of control if they don't keep an eye on everything. It is not long before these on-the-go, high-energy people turn into relational terrorists. When they are irritated, other people keep their distance. This sad state of affairs is a revelation that these believers have not spent much time "in the sun."

1. Write out Matthew 11:28-30 in the spaces below.

   _____

   _____

   _____

   _____

   _____

   _____

Jesus made it quite clear in the passage you just wrote out that a man who spends time learning of Him will be a man known for the peace in his soul. Prayerful reflection on God's wisdom, power, and sovereignty quiets the heart. A person without peace—constantly agitated and restless—does not know God well.

2. Check the statement below which best describes you.

   ☐ I understand what you mean, but I honestly don't know that I have ever really been satisfied—filled with joy and peace—just because of something I learned about God.

   ☐ I have known that kind of satisfied contentment at some time in the past, but I have to confess that it hasn't been an ongoing reality for me.

   ☐ I know what the psalmist was talking about when he said, "O taste and see that the Lord is good" (Psalm 34:8). I regularly experience God in this way and find my greatest joy and peace come from what God is showing me about Himself in His Word.

Centuries ago the prophet Isaiah promised that the man who would "seek . . . the Lord while he may be found" would "go out with *joy*, and be led forth with *peace*" (Isaiah 55:6, 12). Illuminated truth, surging with an unspeakable joy and unquenchable peace, totally satisfies the believer. How can it be otherwise—He has seen God!

3. Memorize Philippians 2:8-10 (Memory Card 53).

And being found in fashion as a man, he humbled himself, and became obedient unto death, even the death of the cross. Wherefore God also hath highly exalted him, and given him a name which is above every name: that at the name of Jesus every knee should bow, of things in heaven, and things in earth, and things under the earth;

4. Memorize Philippians 2:11-12 (Memory Card 54).

And that every tongue should confess that Jesus Christ is Lord, to the glory of God the Father. Wherefore, my beloved, as ye have always obeyed, not as in my presence only, but now much more in my absence, work out your own salvation with fear and trembling.

5. Describe a time when the Holy Spirit illuminated your mind with truth and you saw the beauty and wonder of it and were filled with joy and peace.

_____

_____

_____

_____

_____

To complete this checkpoint, you must read all the text, fill in the blanks, and memorize Philippians 2:8-10 and 2:11-12.

☐ Text read............................Date completed: _____ Initials: _____

☐ Blanks filled in ....Date completed: _____ Initials: _____

☐ Philippians 2:8-10......................Date completed: _____ Initials: _____

☐ Philippians 2:11-12..................Date completed: _____ Initials: _____

I have completed Checkpoint 4.

Your name	Date
Group Leader's name	Date

CHECKPOINT 5 – EVIDENCES OF EXPOSURE TO GOD, CONTINUED

Illuminated Truth Brings Great Desire to Serve God to the Believer

When God's Spirit illuminates the mind with truth, in addition to being moved *intellectually* and *emotionally*, the believer is shown the *urgency* and the *responsibility* of the truth. He cries, *"This is compelling; I must do it!"* He is energized and motivated. He immediately wishes to become a witness of these things. He has something to testify about—he has seen God! The prophet Isaiah, when he saw God, exclaimed, "Here am I; send me" (Isaiah 6:8). The apostle Paul, upon beholding the glory of God, asked, "Lord, what wilt thou have me to do?" (Acts 9:6).

Chris's response at camp, upon seeing the Lord's humility and obedience was to humble himself in repentance and ponder how Christ's humility would look if manifested into whatever service for others he could find around him. The attitude of willing service is the natural result of seeing the glory of God. There is no grudging service here—no clock-watching laborers—only a burning passion of the believer to "present [his body] a living sacrifice, holy, acceptable unto God." He feels it is his "reasonable service" (Romans 12:1). How could it be otherwise—he has seen God!

1. **Memorize Philippians 2:13-14 (Memory Card 55).**

    For it is God which worketh in you both to will and to do of his good pleasure. Do all things without murmurings and disputings.

2. **Memorize Philippians 2:15-16 (Memory Card 56).**

   That ye may be blameless and harmless, the sons of God, without rebuke, in the midst of a crooked and perverse nation, among whom ye shine as lights in the world; holding forth the word of life; that I may rejoice in the day of Christ, that I have not run in vain, neither laboured in vain.

3. Describe a time when God's Spirit illuminated your mind with truth and, because you saw the urgency and responsibility of the truth, your response was essentially, "This is compelling; I must do it."

   _____

   _____

   _____

   _____

This Is Revival!

This effect of illuminated truth upon the heart of a believer is the essence of revival. Just to summarize, those evidences of exposure to God are that illuminated truth moves the believer …

1. Intellectually: He sees the *validity* of the truth and responds, "*This is right; I must believe it!*"

2. Emotionally: He sees the *beauty* of the truth and responds, "*This is wonderful; I must praise it!*"

3. Volitionally: He sees the *urgency* of the truth and responds, "*This is compelling; I must do it!*"

A man moved in this manner by what he is seeing of God is being revived. Others cannot help noticing the profound change. Those around him see his "light so shin[ing] before men, that they . . . see [his] good works, and glorify [his] Father which is in heaven" (Matthew 5:16). The change in him is the direct work of the Spirit of God upon the soul of a man who is seeking God in His Word.

126

Revival, then, does not come when God's people merely start doing right; it comes when God's people start seeing God.

4. According to what you have learned in this unit's study, why do you suppose we are not seeing more revival among believers?

_____

_____

_____

_____

Take a Hike!

Believers must take the time and effort to hike into the forest of God's Word to harvest the logs of truth from that massive timberland. They must by reflection split the logs and stack them in the fireplace of their own heart while they pray for illumination from God to set the logs ablaze. The resulting fire will provide the light that directs their paths and the heart that fuels their passion for God.

Unfortunately, most people accommodate only a few sticks of kindling from their pastor's Sunday sermons—not because he doesn't present some great truths from God's Word but because they reflect little upon those truths, even during the message. Even when God *does* ignite those splinters of truth, their fire blazes but momentarily because there is so little truth for the Spirit to burn.

Solomon's burden in Proverbs 2 is that men would earnestly and diligently search for truth. He says that the man who will do so will "find the knowledge of God" (2:5). He is the one who God says will "*receive* my words, and *hide* my commandments" (2:1). He will "*incline* [his] ear" and "*apply* [his] heart" (2:2). He is the one who "*criest* after knowledge, and *liftest* up [his] voice for understanding" (2:3). He "*seekest* [wisdom] as silver, and *searchest* for her as for hid treasure" (2:4).

This is no casual "I'll-pursue-God-if-I-have-the-time-and-if-I-remember-to-do-it" attitude. It is the wholehearted pursuit of God that is rewarded with a view of God Himself!

To complete this checkpoint, you must read all the text, fill in the blanks, and memorize Philippians 2:13-14 and 2:15-16.

☐ Text read...Date completed: _____ Initials: _____

☐ Blanks filled in ....Date completed: _____ Initials: _____

☐ Philippians 2:13-14 ....Date completed: _____ Initials: _____

☐ Philippians 2:15-16 ....Date completed: _____ Initials: _____

I have completed Checkpoint 5.

_____   _____
Your name   Date

_____   _____
Group Leader's name   Date

CHECKPOINT 6 – JOURNAL WORK

To complete this checkpoint you must journal ten days in a row.

I have completed Checkpoint 6.

_____   _____
Your name   Date

_____   _____
Group Leader's name   Date

CHECKPOINT 7 – CHURCH ATTENDANCE

To complete this checkpoint, you must do the following:

1. Attend two or more church services within one week. They can be the Sunday morning worship service, a Sunday school class, a

Sunday evening service, or a midweek service (sometimes called "prayer meeting").

2. Fill in the information below, and have a pastor of the church sign the proper blank below.

Name of the church: _____

Check the services you attended:

☐ Sunday school

☐ Sunday morning worship service

☐ Sunday evening service

☐ Midweek service

☐ Other (explain): _____

Pastor's signature: _____

I have completed Checkpoint 7.

Your name _____ Date _____

Group Leader's name _____ Date _____

CHECKPOINT 8 – WRITTEN REPORT ON "CHRISTLIKENESS"

To complete this checkpoint, write a one-page paper explaining the important truths you have learned in this lesson. To write the paper you will need to review your answers to remind yourself of what you have learned. Grammar and spelling are not an issue. Do the best you can, asking God to help you understand the importance of learning the process of how we grow and change.

I have completed Checkpoint 8.

_____   _____
Your name   Date

_____   _____
Group Leader's name   Date

CHECKPOINT 9 — SERVICE OPPORTUNITY

An important part of Christian living is serving God and others. To complete this checkpoint, you must ask your *Freedom That Lasts* director or your pastor to once again assign you some area of service for the church or for someone else. It may be an assignment to clean something at the church, to help someone with a special need, to help with setup for *Freedom That Lasts* classes, or to assist in some ministry of the church as a helper. In the blanks below, write out what you did at your pastor's or director's request.

_____

_____

_____

_____

I have completed Checkpoint 9.

_____   _____
Your name   Date

_____   _____
Group Leader's name   Date

CONGRATULATIONS!

You have completed the nine checkpoints necessary to finish this unit. The road map towards growth and change into Christlikeness should be clearer to you now.

When you finish all the checkpoints for this unit and your group leader has signed off on them, you will receive your reward at the end of that class. We encourage you to invite your friends and family to witness your accomplishment.

You have also completed the *Student Manual – Level 2: Growing and Changing God's Way*! This has been no small task. It has been the prayer of your program leaders and your pastor that you will become increasingly like Christ.

To continue your growth in Christ's likeness, you must faithfully continue hearing and doing God's Word.

That means continuing your study and memorization of God's Word. *You may wish to get another copy of this student manual and do it all over again.* You will learn much more the second time through. Or you may ask your group leader or *Freedom That Lasts* director if you are ready to go on to the next level.

You will need to continue to put yourself under the teaching of God's Word in your church. And you will profit by regular attendance at your *Freedom That Lasts* classes where you will continue to grow through the fellowship, accountability, and teaching you will find there.

All these things will point you to the forgiving, willing, and only Savior—Jesus Christ. May you grow to love Him, know Him, and become more like Him! May you grow and change God's way!

Appendix A

HOW TO BECOME A CHRISTIAN

A CRUCIAL QUESTION[1]

Let me ask you a personal question. If you were to die today from a terminal illness or in some tragic accident and you were to stand before God, how would you answer God when He asked you this question: "Why should I let you into My heaven?"

Some people might feel that because they have been deeply religious and have obeyed the Ten Commandments[2] most of the time, God should let them into heaven. Others might feel that because they have lived by the Golden Rule[3] and have been honest and moral in their dealings with others, they should be allowed to enter. They are saying essentially that God should allow them to enter heaven because they have been good in some way.

Jesus predicted that many people would come to Him on that day and would say exactly those things. He says that His reply to them will be, "I never knew you: depart from me, ye that [practice sin]" (Matthew 7:23). You see, no matter how many good things we have done, the factor that will keep us out of heaven is our sin.

The Bible makes it clear that "all have sinned, and come short of the glory of God" (Romans 3:23). That means that all of us have lived as if we are important and that God doesn't matter. We instinctively place ourselves first instead of God and turn to our "own way" (Isaiah 53:6).

---

1 Jim Berg, *When Trouble Comes* (Greenville, SC: BJU Press, 2002), 21–27.
2 Exodus 20:3–17.
3 The Golden Rule: "Do unto others as you would have them do unto you" is a paraphrase of Jesus' statement in Matthew 7:12.

Even our effort to get to heaven by being good shows our rebellion against God because He said that there is no way any of us can be good enough to merit heaven.

Every one of us has broken God's Ten Commandments—and have done so many times. He very clearly said that "the wages of sin is [eternal] death" (Romans 6:23). That means that all of us, because of our rebellion of going our own stubborn way in life, deserve the everlasting punishment of hell because of our mutiny against the Creator.

GOOD NEWS!

The good news for us is that eternal life—life in heaven with Jesus Christ forever—is not something we have to earn. It is a gift! Though "the wages of sin is [eternal] death . . . the gift of God is eternal life through Jesus Christ our Lord" (Romans 6:23). That is good news because the Bible also tells us that it is "not by works of righteousness which we have done, but according to his mercy he saved us" (Titus 3:5). God is willing to mercifully give us a gift we cannot earn. He wants to give us eternal life. But that gift must be personally received by us.

Many public meeting halls operate a lost and found area for those who use the facilities. The lost and found staff holds the property until someone comes by, identifies himself as the owner, and claims the item.

Salvation from the eternal punishment of our sins is available to everyone, but we too must personally claim it.

How can salvation be a free gift? Though it is free to us, it cost Jesus Christ everything. You see, our sins against God require that a penalty be paid. Sinning against our Creator is such a great offense that the only just penalty is eternal suffering and separation from God Himself in hell. Hell is the result of God's granting a man his request—"God, leave me alone." We may not realize it, but that is essentially what we say to God every time we reject His way and live life our own way. That is the bad news for the sinner[4]

---

[4]Jesus Himself speaks of hell as a place of literal torment (Luke 16:19-31).

134

The good news is that God loves us and arranged for His own Son to live on this earth to pay the penalty for us. Though Jesus lived in a body like ours, He did not share our sinful and stubborn nature. He lived a sinless life in complete obedience to His Father while on the earth. He qualified—as a perfect sacrificial lamb—to die in our place. Look at these chilling but wonderful words from the Old Testament, which predicted the sacrificial death of Jesus Christ on the cross for us:

> *He was wounded for our transgressions, he was bruised for our iniquities: the chastisement [for] our peace was upon him; and with his stripes we are healed. All we like sheep have gone astray; we have turned every one to his own way; and the Lord hath laid on him the iniquity of us all. (Isaiah. 53:5–6)*

The apostle John states the same thing this way:

> *For God so loved the world, that he gave his only begotten Son, that whosoever believeth in him should not perish, but have everlasting life . . . .He that believeth on him is not condemned: but he that believeth not is condemned already, because he hath not believed in the name of the only begotten Son of God. (John 3:16, 18)*

Jesus' sacrifice of His own blood as the eternal payment for anyone who would believe on Him satisfied the righteous anger of God against our mutiny. All that is left is for us to admit to God that we are indeed hell-deserving sinners, realize that Jesus died in our place and arose from the dead, and then accept the gift of eternal life from God. It is a simple plan—one that even a child can understand. A child will cry out for help to the person he believes will help him. A sinner who wants the gift of eternal life can come to Jesus Christ by praying a prayer like this:

> Lord Jesus, I realize that I am a sinner. I have not obeyed You. I have gone my own way many times. Since You are perfect and Your heaven is perfect, I realize that even one sin would disqualify me from heaven.[5] I repent of my sin and ask Your forgiveness. I accept Your gift of eternal life. I want Your substitutionary death to be applied to my sin account.[6] Cleanse me from my sin and make me one of Your own children.[7] Thank you for loving me and for saving me.

It is our prayer that if you do not know Jesus Christ as your personal Savior from sin, you will repent of your sin and come to Christ today. He is waiting to hear from you.

If you want to know more about how to become a child of God and how you can have your sins forgiven, please see your group leader, Freedom That Lasts director, or your pastor.

> *For whosoever shall call upon the name of the Lord shall be saved. (Romans 10:13).*

---

[5] James 2:10.
[6] 2 Corinthians 5:21.
[7] John 1:12.

Appendix B

CHOOSING THE RIGHT KIND OF CHURCH

In Acts 2:42 the Bible says that the new Christians "continued steadfastly in the apostles' doctrine [solid biblical teaching] and fellowship." These two elements are essential to your Christian growth. God has established the local church as the means to meet these needs. Some today would scorn meeting together in an organized fashion. It is true that some churches have nothing to offer the believer who is seeking to be fed from God's Word, but God has not abandoned this institution.

Of course, a Christian must use caution in selecting the right kind of church. The Bible gives definite instructions as to the kind of church a Christian should fellowship with.

Acts 21:8–14—It must have the gospel as its central message. This means the pastor and teachers will continually be telling their listeners how to be saved and may offer regular times of "invitation" when a person can get help on how to be saved.

The pastor will also bring the truths of the gospel to bear upon believers as well so they can rejoice in Jesus' work on the cross and live in the freedom from sin's bondage that Jesus promised.

1 Timothy 3:1–13—Its leaders should meet God's qualifications of dedication and holy living.

2 Corinthians 6:14, 17—It should be independent of ungodly alliances and associations with religious organizations that do not obey the Bible or that do not hold it to be entirely true.

Churches that meet these qualifications often describe themselves as "independent," "fundamental," or "evangelistic." Once you find the right church, attend every service and get involved in its ministry outreaches.

God has raised up churches like these to strengthen you spiritually through the Bible preaching and teaching and the fellowship with other believers who love and obey the Bible.

Appendix C

A PLAN FOR A DAILY QUIET TIME WITH GOD

Nothing will help you grow more and build your relationship with God more quickly than a daily quiet time. This is a time when you meet with God.

Once you are consistent in journaling using the *Freedom That Lasts Spiritual Life Journal*, you may want to include other components in your daily quiet time with God. This article will give you some additional ideas of what to do.

Please don't be discouraged if you can't do everything in the plan at the beginning of your walk with God. In fact, don't be discouraged if you can't do everything in the pages of the *Freedom That Lasts Spiritual Life Journal*. We all have to take baby steps before we can walk—then jog—then run a marathon.

PRINCIPLES FOR GETTING STARTED

Remember the following points as you begin to make this a part of your daily schedule.

Establish a regular time. Many Christians find that early morning is best since their first thoughts can be of spiritual things (Psalm 5:3).

Get alone. Shut yourself up in a room away from the distractions of other people, if possible (Matthew 6:6).

Have a pen and your *Spiritual Life Journal* ready. Proverbs 10:14 says, "Wise men [store] up knowledge." Be ready to write down anything God points out to you from His Word. As you learn more each day in the months ahead you will find that your daily journal pages will not be able to hold all the things you want to write down.

You can then purchase a separate notebook in which you write down the many lessons you are learning. To begin with, the daily journal pages will be enough, however.

Include the following elements in your quiet time:

1. Bible Reading

Pray before you begin reading. Ask God to show you something just for you (Psalm 119:18).

Follow a Bible reading schedule so that your reading is not haphazard. See the reading schedule for the New Testament in Appendix D on page 144 of this student manual. Try to read one assignment a day and write the date in the blank when you finish the reading.

Include the chapter of Proverbs that corresponds to the day of the month (e.g., read Proverbs 15 on the fifteenth day of the month).

Read until God points out something especially for you. Jot down the verse and your immediate thoughts about it. As you read, God will convict you of sins in your life.

Write down your decision to forsake these sins. In your prayer time, confess these sins to God and ask for power to overcome them. God uses His Word to cleanse us as a standard against which we can compare ourselves to see our needs and our sins.

Thank God for what He has shown you in your reading.

Share these special verses and insights with others (1 John 1:3).

2. Meditation: The MAP Method

Find a portion of Scripture relevant to your problem or find one that deals with a Bible truth you wish to master. Always meditate on Scripture that God's Spirit "highlights" as you are reading His Word.

Memorize the Passage

Memorizing often occurs automatically if the passage is studied intensely enough in the next step. During temptation you must know exactly what God has said word for word. Merely having a general idea about what is right is not enough when dealing with the deceptive nature of your own heart. A man who cannot remember God's exact words is in danger of leaning on his "own understanding" (Proverbs 3:5).

Read carefully the next article, "How to Memorize Scripture," to give you some ideas for committing Bible verses to memory.

A nalyze the Passage

Study the passage, asking the Holy Spirit to give you a thorough understanding of its message. You can do an intensive study of the passage by listing the major words of the verses and then using an English dictionary to find out the meaning for each word. If possible, look up each word in a Greek or Hebrew dictionary or check the meaning of each word in Strong's Exhaustive Concordance. Once you are sure of each word's meaning, put the passage in your own words (i.e., paraphrase it).

A more extensive study would involve using a commentary or a good study Bible to help you understand more about who wrote the passage, to whom it was written, and why it was written.[8] Most important, pray that God will illuminate your understanding. Ask Him to teach you what He wants you to know from the Scriptures.

P ersonalize the Passage

Plan concrete changes in your life that are consistent with your understanding of the passage. Such plans would include schedules, steps, and details. Ask yourself, "When have I failed to obey this truth in the past? When am I likely to meet a temptation again? What should be the godly response the next time I am tempted?" Think through this "game plan" thoroughly and in advance of the next temptation.

Use the passage in a personal prayer to God. For example, a person meditating on James 4:1–11 may begin a prayer this way: "Lord, you

---

[8]Every growing believer should own and use a good study Bible. A study Bible includes many historical and explanatory notes and cross-references which help you understand what the Bible text is saying. Ask your group leader, Freedom That Lasts director, or pastor for a recommendation. Consider the Ryrie Study Bible, the MacArthur Study Bible, or the Life Application Study Bible. Each is available in various translations.

tell me here in James 4:1 that the conflict I am having with John is the result of my own lusts—my desires to have something my way. I know that isn't pleasing to You. Instead of responding in anger to John, I need Your help and grace, which You promise in James 4:6, where You say that You resist the proud but give grace to the humble. Help me to humble myself and not to insist on my own way. I want to allow You to lift me up in Your time."

3. Prayer

Our prayers to God should contain a balance of praise and thanksgiving, confession, supplication (asking), and submission. You can keep this balance by letting the acronym "PRAY" remind you of these elements during your prayer times. Memorize the Scripture passages following each element and pray them back to God sincerely from your heart.

Praise God for who He is (Psalm 8; 1 Chronicles 29:11–13) and for what He has done (Psalm 100:4).

Repent of your sin (1 John 1:9; Psalm 32:1–5).

Ask God to provide what you need (Matthew 7:7–8; Philippians 4:6).

Yield yourself to God to change and use as He sees fit today (Romans 6:13; James 4:7).

A balanced prayer life includes times of fellowship with God when we spend time praising Him and times of petition to God for help. Our tendency is to forget the times of adoration and thanksgiving—the times of praise—and to concentrate upon asking God for things. Without the times of praise, however, our prayer life becomes a shallow "give me" time. Praise to God will become easier as you see God answer your requests and as you learn more about the kind of person God is. Of course, this does not mean that every time you pray you must include all four elements, but none of them should be missing from your regular prayer life.

CONCLUSION

Make a daily quiet time a regular part of your life. You will be amazed at the joy and blessing God brings to your life when you develop a relationship with His Son, Jesus Christ—the only source of freedom that lasts!

Appendix D
BIBLE READING SCHEDULE FOR THE NEW TESTAMENT

Date Read

Date Read	Book	Chapters	Date Read	Book	Chapters
_____	Matthew	1–4	_____	Acts	10–11
_____	Matthew	5–7	_____	Acts	12–13
_____	Matthew	8–10	_____	Acts	14–15
_____	Matthew	11–12	_____	Acts	16–18
_____	Matthew	13–14	_____	Acts	19–20
_____	Matthew	15–17	_____	Acts	21–23
_____	Matthew	18–20	_____	Acts	24–26
_____	Matthew	21–22	_____	Acts	27–28
_____	Matthew	23–24	_____	Romans	1–3
_____	Matthew	25–26	_____	Romans	4–7
_____	Matthew	27–28	_____	Romans	8–11
_____	Mark	1–3	_____	Romans	12–16
_____	Mark	4–5	_____	1 Corinthians	1–4
_____	Mark	6–7	_____	1 Corinthians	5–8
_____	Mark	8–9	_____	1 Corinthians	9–11
_____	Mark	10–12	_____	1 Corinthians	12–14
_____	Mark	13–14	_____	1 Corinthians	15–16
_____	Mark	15–16	_____	2 Corinthians	1–5
_____	Luke	1–2	_____	2 Corinthians	6–10
_____	Luke	3–4	_____	2 Corinthians	11–13
_____	Luke	5–6	_____	Galatians	1–4
_____	Luke	7–8	_____	Galatians 5–Ephesians 3	
_____	Luke	9–10	_____	Ephesians	4–6
_____	Luke	11–12	_____	Philippians	1–4
_____	Luke	13–15	_____	Colossians	1–4
_____	Luke	16–18	_____	1 Thessalonians	1–5
_____	Luke	19–20	_____	2 Thessalonians	1–3
_____	Luke	21–22	_____	1 Timothy	1–6
_____	Luke	23–24	_____	2 Timothy	1–4
_____	John	1–2	_____	Titus–Philemon	
_____	John	3–4	_____	Hebrews	1–4
_____	John	5–6	_____	Hebrews	5–8
_____	John	7–8	_____	Hebrews	9–10
_____	John	9–10	_____	Hebrews	11–13
_____	John	11–12	_____	James	1–5
_____	John	13–15	_____	1 Peter	1–5
_____	John	16–18	_____	2 Peter	1–3
_____	John	19–21	_____	1 John	1–5
_____	Acts	1–2	_____	2 John–Revelation 2	
_____	Acts	3–5	_____	Revelation	3–8
_____	Acts	6–7	_____	Revelation	9–13
_____	Acts	8–9	_____	Revelation	14–18
			_____	Revelation	19–22

Appendix E
VERSES FOR VICTORY

Forgiveness	1 John 1:9	Psalm 103:12	1 John 2:1–2
Patience	Hebrews 10:36	James 1:2–4	1 Peter 2:20
Strength	Ephesians 3:16	Phillipians 4:13	Ephesians 6:10–11
Lust (1)	2 Timothy 2:22	1 John 2:15–17	1 Peter 2:11
Lust (2)	Matthew 5:28	Romans 13:14	James 1:5
Priorities	Matthew 6:33	Acts 20:24	Phillipians 3:8
Self-Discipline	Ecclesiastes 5:4	Luke 9:23	James 1:19–20
Pleasing God	Matthew 6:5,6	Ephesians 6:6–7	Colossians 3:23
Christian Walk	Ephesians 4:1-2	Ephesians 5:2	Ephesians 5:8–9
Temptation	1 Corinthians 10:13	James 4:7	Romans 6:11–13
Peace	John 14:27	John 16:33	Phillipians 4:6–7
Wise Counsel	Proverbs 11:14	Proverbs 12:15	Proverbs 1:5
Courage	Psalm 31:24	Psalm 34:4	Proverbs 29:25
Pride (1)	Proverbs 16:18	Romans 12:3	James 4:6
Pride (2)	Obadiah 1:4	Matthew 20:26–27	1 Corinthians 4:7
Love	Deuteronomy 6:5	John 13:35	John 15:13
Worldliness	Romans 12:2	Colossians 3:2	James 4:4
Tongue	James 3:6	Ephesians 4:29	Proverbs 10:19
Lying	Psalm 120:2	Psalm 101:7	Proverbs 19:5
Stealing	Ephesians 4:28	Proverbs 30:8–9	Exodus 20:15
Suffering	Romans 8:18	Phillipians 1:29	1 Peter 2:21
Church Attendance	Psalm 122:1	Matthew 18:20	Hebrews 10:25
Evil Thoughts	2 Corinthians 10:5	Phillipians 4:8	Ephesians 5:12
Critical Spirit	1 Corinthians 10:10	Phillipians 2:14	James 5:9
Strong Drink	Isaiah 5:11	Habakkuk 2:15	Romans 14:21
Guidance	Proverbs 3:5,6	Psalm 32:8	Proverbs 1:23
Forgiving Others	Matt. 5:44	Mark 11:25	Ephesians 4:32
Knowing God	Jer. 9:23–24	John 17:3	Phillipians 3:8,10
Assurance	John 3:36	John 10:28	1 John 5:13

As you find other areas of need and Verses for Victory, write them in the spaces below.

Appendix F

HOW TO MEMORIZE SCRIPTURE

Memorizing for most of us is not easy at first. It is hard to make something "stick" in our minds.

Tar is a black sticky substance that can help us remember how to make what we memorize stick. Just think T. A. R.

Think it through

And

Repeat it often.

Think it through

Something is easier to memorize if we understand it. If the meaning of the verse you are memorizing is not clear to you, ask your group leader, your pastor, or another mature Christian to explain it to you. This will be a great help to you as you memorize it.

And

Repeat it often.

Evangelist Ron Hood has developed a Bible memory plan that has met with great success.[1] It helps you repeat the verse enough times so that you actually learn it without too much mental strain.

You must start with an understanding of the verse first—as discussed above. Next you write the verse on a note card—the verses and

---

[1] Adapted from *How to Successfully Memorize and Review Scripture*, by Ron Hood, (Greenville, SC: Spiritual Success Institute, Inc., www.RonHood.org, 1974). Used with Permission.

definitions used in this student manual are printed in the back of this book. See **Example 1.**

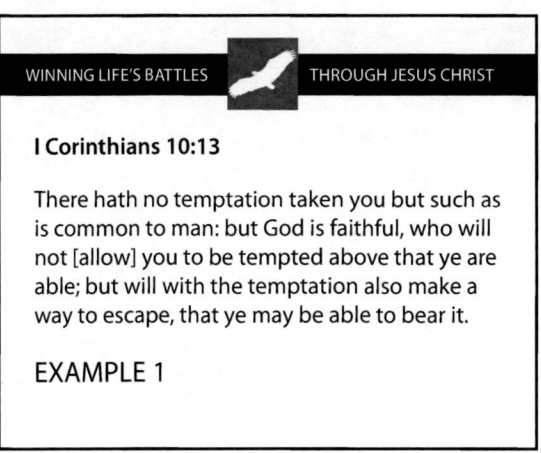

To memorize the verse, say it twenty-five times the first day, twenty times the second day, fifteen times the third day, ten times the fourth day, and five times the fifth day.

Once you get to this point review the card every day for forty-five days, then review it once a week for seven weeks, and then monthly.

This sounds like a lot of repetition, but that's the point! Remember T.A.R.? You must "Repeat it often."

This also sounds like a lot of bookkeeping, but it is simpler than you think. The secret is to keep track of your repetitions on the back of the card.

```
1st 5 days                          Next 45 days

Day 1   JHT JHT JHT JHT JHT      1 2 3 4 5 6 7 8
Day 2   JHT JHT JHT JHT          9 10 11 12 13 14
Day 3   JHT JHT JHT            15 16 17 18 19 20 21
Day 4   JHT JHT             22 23 24 25 26 27 28 29
Day 5   JHT             30 31 32 33 34 35 36 37 38
                    39 40 41 42 43 44 45

Once a week for seven weeks: 1 2 3 4 5 6 7
Once a month: Jan Feb Mar Apr May Jun Jul
Aug Sep Oct Nov Dec

EXAMPLE 2
```

The back of the card in **Example 2** shows you that the user said the verse twenty-five times the first day. Every time he read the verse concentrating on what it means, he traced over a tick mark on the back. After each four tick marks he traced over a diagonal mark to show he did it five times.

The next day he did the same thing except he read it over twenty times, On day three he said the verse fifteen times, and on day four he said it ten times. That is as far as he has gone so far.

Notice **Example 3** where the user has completed the work for day one through day five and has said the verse daily for seven days at this time. Notice the diagonal marks he has made on days one through seven under the heading "Next 45 days." He will continue to say the verse once a day until he has done so for forty-five days. He will cross out the next number on every day that he says the verse.

```
┌─────────────────────────────────────────────────────┐
│  1st 5 days                         Next 45 days       │
│                                                        │
│  Day 1    JHT JHT JHT JHT JHT      1 2 3 4 5 6 7 8     │
│  Day 2    JHT JHT JHT JHT          9 10 11 12 13 14    │
│  Day 3    JHT JHT JHT           15 16 17 18 19 20 21   │
│  Day 4    JHT JHT           22 23 24 25 26 27 28 29    │
│  Day 5    JHT           30 31 32 33 34 35 36 37 38     │
│                      39 40 41 42 43 44 45              │
│                                                        │
│  Once a week for seven weeks: 1 2 3 4 5 6 7            │
│  Once a month: Jan Feb Mar Apr May Jun Jul             │
│  Aug Sep Oct Nov Dec                                   │
│  EXAMPLE 3                                             │
└─────────────────────────────────────────────────────┘
```

Once you have said the Memory Card daily for forty-five days, put it on a pile of cards on your dresser or somewhere near your Bible in a "weekly stack."

Once a week, perhaps on Sunday afternoon, go through this stack and review the verses you have learned. Check off what week it is for that Memory Card in the section entitled, "Once a week for seven weeks." Notice in **Example 4** that the user has completed day one through day five, has said the Memory Card for forty-five days, and now has been reviewing it once a week for three weeks.

```
┌─────────────────────────────────────────────────┐
│  1st 5 days                         Next 45 days  │
│                                                   │
│  Day 1  J̶H̶T̶ J̶H̶T̶ J̶H̶T̶ J̶H̶T̶ J̶H̶T̶      1̶ 2̶ 3̶ 4̶ 5̶ 6̶ 7̶ 8̶     │
│  Day 2  J̶H̶T̶ J̶H̶T̶ J̶H̶T̶ J̶H̶T̶          9̶ 1̶0̶ 1̶1̶ 1̶2̶ 1̶3̶ 1̶4̶    │
│  Day 3  J̶H̶T̶ J̶H̶T̶ J̶H̶T̶              1̶5̶ 1̶6̶ 1̶7̶ 1̶8̶ 1̶9̶ 2̶0̶ 2̶1̶  │
│  Day 4  J̶H̶T̶ J̶H̶T̶              2̶2̶ 2̶3̶ 2̶4̶ 2̶5̶ 2̶6̶ 2̶7̶ 2̶8̶ 2̶9̶   │
│  Day 5  J̶H̶T̶              3̶0̶ 3̶1̶ 3̶2̶ 3̶3̶ 3̶4̶ 3̶5̶ 3̶6̶ 3̶7̶ 3̶8̶    │
│                      3̶9̶ 4̶0̶ 4̶1̶ 4̶2̶ 4̶3̶ 4̶4̶ 4̶5̶               │
│                                                   │
│  Once a week for seven weeks: 1̶ 2̶ 3̶ 4 5 6 7      │
│  Once a month: Jan Feb Mar Apr May Jun Jul        │
│  Aug Sep Oct Nov Dec                              │
│  EXAMPLE 4                                        │
└─────────────────────────────────────────────────┘
```

Once you have said the verse weekly for seven weeks, put it in a "monthly stack" to review once a month from then on. When you review the verse for that month circle the name of that month. If you start reviewing the verse in April, circle April and when you have finished December, circle January when you review it the next month. It doesn't matter what month you put the card in your "monthly stack." Just continue reviewing monthly for at least a year—and longer if you need to.

Notice in **Example 5** that the user has reviewed the card for April and May already.

```
┌─────────────────────────────────────────────────┐
│  1st 5 days                         Next 45 days  │
│                                                   │
│  Day 1  J̶H̶T̶ J̶H̶T̶ J̶H̶T̶ J̶H̶T̶ J̶H̶T̶      1̶ 2̶ 3̶ 4̶ 5̶ 6̶ 7̶ 8̶     │
│  Day 2  J̶H̶T̶ J̶H̶T̶ J̶H̶T̶ J̶H̶T̶          9̶ 1̶0̶ 1̶1̶ 1̶2̶ 1̶3̶ 1̶4̶    │
│  Day 3  J̶H̶T̶ J̶H̶T̶ J̶H̶T̶              1̶5̶ 1̶6̶ 1̶7̶ 1̶8̶ 1̶9̶ 2̶0̶ 2̶1̶  │
│  Day 4  J̶H̶T̶ J̶H̶T̶              2̶2̶ 2̶3̶ 2̶4̶ 2̶5̶ 2̶6̶ 2̶7̶ 2̶8̶ 2̶9̶   │
│  Day 5  J̶H̶T̶              3̶0̶ 3̶1̶ 3̶2̶ 3̶3̶ 3̶4̶ 3̶5̶ 3̶6̶ 3̶7̶ 3̶8̶    │
│                      3̶9̶ 4̶0̶ 4̶1̶ 4̶2̶ 4̶3̶ 4̶4̶ 4̶5̶               │
│                                                   │
│  Once a week for seven weeks: 1̶ 2̶ 3̶ 4̶ 5̶ 6̶ 7     │
│  Once a month: Jan Feb Mar (Apr)(May) Jun Jul     │
│  Aug Sep Oct Nov Dec                              │
│  EXAMPLE 5                                        │
└─────────────────────────────────────────────────┘
```

WINNING LIFE'S BATTLES  THROUGH JESUS CHRIST

1. Mark 7:21-23

For from within, out of the heart of men, proceed evil thoughts, adulteries, fornications, murders, thefts, covetousness, deceit, [sensuality, envy, slander], pride, foolishness: All these evil things come from within, and defile the man.

1st 5 days   **Next 45 days**

Day 1 ||||| ||||| ||||| ||||| ||||| 1 2 3 4 5 6 7 8
Day 2 ||||| ||||| ||||| ||||| 9 10 11 12 13 14
Day 3 ||||| ||||| ||||| 15 16 17 18 19 20 21
Day 4 ||||| ||||| 22 23 24 25 26 27 28 29
Day 5 ||||| 30 31 32 33 34 35 36 37 38
         39 40 41 42 43 44 45

Once a week for seven weeks: 1 2 3 4 5 6 7
Once a month: Jan Feb Mar Apr May Jun Jul Aug Sep Oct Nov Dec

---

WINNING LIFE'S BATTLES THROUGH JESUS CHRIST

2. 2 Corinthians 5:17

Therefore if any man be in Christ, he is a new creature: old things are passed away; behold, all things are become new.

1st 5 days   **Next 45 days**

Day 1 ||||| ||||| ||||| ||||| ||||| 1 2 3 4 5 6 7 8
Day 2 ||||| ||||| ||||| ||||| 9 10 11 12 13 14
Day 3 ||||| ||||| ||||| 15 16 17 18 19 20 21
Day 4 ||||| ||||| 22 23 24 25 26 27 28 29
Day 5 ||||| 30 31 32 33 34 35 36 37 38
         39 40 41 42 43 44 45

Once a week for seven weeks: 1 2 3 4 5 6 7
Once a month: Jan Feb Mar Apr May Jun Jul Aug Sep Oct Nov Dec

---

WINNING LIFE'S BATTLES THROUGH JESUS CHRIST

3. Galatians 5:22-23

But the fruit of the Spirit is love, joy, peace, longsuffering, gentleness, goodness, faith, meekness, temperance….

1st 5 days   **Next 45 days**

Day 1 ||||| ||||| ||||| ||||| ||||| 1 2 3 4 5 6 7 8
Day 2 ||||| ||||| ||||| ||||| 9 10 11 12 13 14
Day 3 ||||| ||||| ||||| 15 16 17 18 19 20 21
Day 4 ||||| ||||| 22 23 24 25 26 27 28 29
Day 5 ||||| 30 31 32 33 34 35 36 37 38
         39 40 41 42 43 44 45

Once a week for seven weeks: 1 2 3 4 5 6 7
Once a month: Jan Feb Mar Apr May Jun Jul Aug Sep Oct Nov Dec

---

WINNING LIFE'S BATTLES THROUGH JESUS CHRIST

4. Galatians 5:16

This I say then, Walk in the Spirit, and ye shall not fulfil the lust of the flesh.

1st 5 days   **Next 45 days**

Day 1 ||||| ||||| ||||| ||||| ||||| 1 2 3 4 5 6 7 8
Day 2 ||||| ||||| ||||| ||||| 9 10 11 12 13 14
Day 3 ||||| ||||| ||||| 15 16 17 18 19 20 21
Day 4 ||||| ||||| 22 23 24 25 26 27 28 29
Day 5 ||||| 30 31 32 33 34 35 36 37 38
         39 40 41 42 43 44 45

Once a week for seven weeks: 1 2 3 4 5 6 7
Once a month: Jan Feb Mar Apr May Jun Jul Aug Sep Oct Nov Dec

1st 5 days	Next 45 days

5. Definition of Sanctification

Sanctification is that process whereby the Spirit of God uses the Word of God to make us like the Son of God amidst the circumstances we face in the providence of God.

Day 1 ㅐ카 ㅐ카 ㅐ카 ㅐ카 ㅐ카   1 2 3 4 5 6 7 8
Day 2 ㅐ카 ㅐ카 ㅐ카 ㅐ카   9 10 11 12 13 14
Day 3 ㅐ카 ㅐ카 ㅐ카   15 16 17 18 19 20 21
Day 4 ㅐ카 ㅐ카   22 23 24 25 26 27 28 29
Day 5 ㅐ카   30 31 32 33 34 35 36 37 38
39 40 41 42 43 44 45

Once a week for seven weeks: 1 2 3 4 5 6 7
Once a month: Jan Feb Mar Apr May Jun Jul Aug Sep Oct Nov Dec

---

1st 5 days	Next 45 days

6. Definition of Discipleship

Discipleship is helping another believer make biblical change toward Christlikeness.

Day 1 ㅐ카 ㅐ카 ㅐ카 ㅐ카 ㅐ카   1 2 3 4 5 6 7 8
Day 2 ㅐ카 ㅐ카 ㅐ카 ㅐ카   9 10 11 12 13 14
Day 3 ㅐ카 ㅐ카 ㅐ카   15 16 17 18 19 20 21
Day 4 ㅐ카 ㅐ카   22 23 24 25 26 27 28 29
Day 5 ㅐ카   30 31 32 33 34 35 36 37 38
39 40 41 42 43 44 45

Once a week for seven weeks: 1 2 3 4 5 6 7
Once a month: Jan Feb Mar Apr May Jun Jul Aug Sep Oct Nov Dec

---

1st 5 days	Next 45 days

7. 1 Timothy 4:15-16

Meditate upon these things; give thyself wholly to them: that thy profiting may appear to all. Take heed unto thyself, and unto the doctrine; continue in them: for in doing this thou shalt both [help] thyself, and them that hear thee.

Day 1 ㅐ카 ㅐ카 ㅐ카 ㅐ카 ㅐ카   1 2 3 4 5 6 7 8
Day 2 ㅐ카 ㅐ카 ㅐ카 ㅐ카   9 10 11 12 13 14
Day 3 ㅐ카 ㅐ카 ㅐ카   15 16 17 18 19 20 21
Day 4 ㅐ카 ㅐ카   22 23 24 25 26 27 28 29
Day 5 ㅐ카   30 31 32 33 34 35 36 37 38
39 40 41 42 43 44 45

Once a week for seven weeks: 1 2 3 4 5 6 7
Once a month: Jan Feb Mar Apr May Jun Jul Aug Sep Oct Nov Dec

---

1st 5 days	Next 45 days

8. 1 Corinthians 15:22

For as in Adam all die, even so in Christ shall all be made alive.

Day 1 ㅐ카 ㅐ카 ㅐ카 ㅐ카 ㅐ카   1 2 3 4 5 6 7 8
Day 2 ㅐ카 ㅐ카 ㅐ카 ㅐ카   9 10 11 12 13 14
Day 3 ㅐ카 ㅐ카 ㅐ카   15 16 17 18 19 20 21
Day 4 ㅐ카 ㅐ카   22 23 24 25 26 27 28 29
Day 5 ㅐ카   30 31 32 33 34 35 36 37 38
39 40 41 42 43 44 45

Once a week for seven weeks: 1 2 3 4 5 6 7
Once a month: Jan Feb Mar Apr May Jun Jul Aug Sep Oct Nov Dec

9. Romans 7:25

I thank God through Jesus Christ our Lord. So then with the mind I myself serve the law of God; but with the flesh the law of sin.

1st 5 days   **Next 45 days**

Day 1   ~~JHT~~ ~~JHT~~ ~~JHT~~ ~~JHT~~ ~~JHT~~   1 2 3 4 5 6 7 8
Day 2   ~~JHT~~ ~~JHT~~ ~~JHT~~ ~~JHT~~   9 10 11 12 13 14
Day 3   ~~JHT~~ ~~JHT~~ ~~JHT~~   15 16 17 18 19 20 21
Day 4   ~~JHT~~ ~~JHT~~   22 23 24 25 26 27 28 29
Day 5   ~~JHT~~   30 31 32 33 34 35 36 37 38
       39 40 41 42 43 44 45

Once a week for seven weeks: 1 2 3 4 5 6 7
Once a month: Jan Feb Mar Apr May Jun Jul Aug Sep Oct Nov Dec

---

10. Matthew 26:41

Watch and pray, that ye enter not into temptation: the spirit, indeed, is willing, but the flesh is weak.

1st 5 days   **Next 45 days**

Day 1   ~~JHT~~ ~~JHT~~ ~~JHT~~ ~~JHT~~ ~~JHT~~   1 2 3 4 5 6 7 8
Day 2   ~~JHT~~ ~~JHT~~ ~~JHT~~ ~~JHT~~   9 10 11 12 13 14
Day 3   ~~JHT~~ ~~JHT~~ ~~JHT~~   15 16 17 18 19 20 21
Day 4   ~~JHT~~ ~~JHT~~   22 23 24 25 26 27 28 29
Day 5   ~~JHT~~   30 31 32 33 34 35 36 37 38
       39 40 41 42 43 44 45

Once a week for seven weeks: 1 2 3 4 5 6 7
Once a month: Jan Feb Mar Apr May Jun Jul Aug Sep Oct Nov Dec

---

11. 1 Corinthians 10:12-13

Wherefore let him that thinketh he standeth take heed lest he fall. There hath no temptation taken you but such as is common to man: but God is faithful, who will not suffer you to be tempted above that ye are able; but will with the temptation provide a way to escape, that ye may be able to bear it.

1st 5 days   **Next 45 days**

Day 1   ~~JHT~~ ~~JHT~~ ~~JHT~~ ~~JHT~~ ~~JHT~~   1 2 3 4 5 6 7 8
Day 2   ~~JHT~~ ~~JHT~~ ~~JHT~~ ~~JHT~~   9 10 11 12 13 14
Day 3   ~~JHT~~ ~~JHT~~ ~~JHT~~   15 16 17 18 19 20 21
Day 4   ~~JHT~~ ~~JHT~~   22 23 24 25 26 27 28 29
Day 5   ~~JHT~~   30 31 32 33 34 35 36 37 38
       39 40 41 42 43 44 45

Once a week for seven weeks: 1 2 3 4 5 6 7
Once a month: Jan Feb Mar Apr May Jun Jul Aug Sep Oct Nov Dec

---

12. Galatians 6:7-9

Be not deceived: God is not mocked: for whatsoever a man soweth, that shall he also reap. For he that soweth to his flesh shall of the flesh reap corruption: but he that soweth to the Spirit shall of the Spirit reap life everlasting. And let us not be weary in well doing: for in due season we shall reap, if we faint not.

1st 5 days   **Next 45 days**

Day 1   ~~JHT~~ ~~JHT~~ ~~JHT~~ ~~JHT~~ ~~JHT~~   1 2 3 4 5 6 7 8
Day 2   ~~JHT~~ ~~JHT~~ ~~JHT~~ ~~JHT~~   9 10 11 12 13 14
Day 3   ~~JHT~~ ~~JHT~~ ~~JHT~~   15 16 17 18 19 20 21
Day 4   ~~JHT~~ ~~JHT~~   22 23 24 25 26 27 28 29
Day 5   ~~JHT~~   30 31 32 33 34 35 36 37 38
       39 40 41 42 43 44 45

Once a week for seven weeks: 1 2 3 4 5 6 7
Once a month: Jan Feb Mar Apr May Jun Jul Aug Sep Oct Nov Dec

WINNING LIFE'S BATTLES   THROUGH JESUS CHRIST

13.   Jeremiah 17:9

The heart is deceitful above all things, and desperately wicked; who can know it?

1st 5 days

Day 1   JHT JHT JHT JHT JHT
Day 2   JHT JHT JHT JHT
Day 3   JHT JHT JHT
Day 4   JHT JHT
Day 5   JHT

Next 45 days

1 2 3 4 5 6 7 8
9 10 11 12 13 14
15 16 17 18 19 20 21
22 23 24 25 26 27 28 29
30 31 32 33 34 35 36 37 38
39 40 41 42 43 44 45

Once a week for seven weeks: 1 2 3 4 5 6 7
Once a month: Jan Feb Mar Apr May Jun Jul Aug Sep Oct Nov Dec

---

WINNING LIFE'S BATTLES   THROUGH JESUS CHRIST

14.   James 1:17

Every good gift and every perfect gift is from above, and cometh down from the Father of lights, with whom is no variableness, neither shadow of turning.

1st 5 days

Day 1   JHT JHT JHT JHT JHT
Day 2   JHT JHT JHT JHT
Day 3   JHT JHT JHT
Day 4   JHT JHT
Day 5   JHT

Next 45 days

1 2 3 4 5 6 7 8
9 10 11 12 13 14
15 16 17 18 19 20 21
22 23 24 25 26 27 28 29
30 31 32 33 34 35 36 37 38
39 40 41 42 43 44 45

Once a week for seven weeks: 1 2 3 4 5 6 7
Once a month: Jan Feb Mar Apr May Jun Jul Aug Sep Oct Nov Dec

---

WINNING LIFE'S BATTLES   THROUGH JESUS CHRIST

15.   1 Peter 5:5

Likewise, ye younger, submit yourselves unto the elder. Yea, all of you be subject one to another, and be clothed with humility: for God resisteth the proud, and giveth grace to the humble.

1st 5 days

Day 1   JHT JHT JHT JHT JHT
Day 2   JHT JHT JHT JHT
Day 3   JHT JHT JHT
Day 4   JHT JHT
Day 5   JHT

Next 45 days

1 2 3 4 5 6 7 8
9 10 11 12 13 14
15 16 17 18 19 20 21
22 23 24 25 26 27 28 29
30 31 32 33 34 35 36 37 38
39 40 41 42 43 44 45

Once a week for seven weeks: 1 2 3 4 5 6 7
Once a month: Jan Feb Mar Apr May Jun Jul Aug Sep Oct Nov Dec

---

WINNING LIFE'S BATTLES   THROUGH JESUS CHRIST

16.   Proverbs 14:12

There is a way which seemeth right unto a man, but the end thereof are the ways of death.

1st 5 days

Day 1   JHT JHT JHT JHT JHT
Day 2   JHT JHT JHT JHT
Day 3   JHT JHT JHT
Day 4   JHT JHT
Day 5   JHT

Next 45 days

1 2 3 4 5 6 7 8
9 10 11 12 13 14
15 16 17 18 19 20 21
22 23 24 25 26 27 28 29
30 31 32 33 34 35 36 37 38
39 40 41 42 43 44 45

Once a week for seven weeks: 1 2 3 4 5 6 7
Once a month: Jan Feb Mar Apr May Jun Jul Aug Sep Oct Nov Dec

17. Proverbs 3:5-6

Trust in the Lord with all thine heart; and lean not unto thine own understanding. In all thy ways acknowledge him, and he shall direct thy paths.

1st 5 days   **Next 45 days**

Day 1   JHT JHT JHT JHT JHT   1 2 3 4 5 6 7 8
Day 2   JHT JHT JHT JHT   9 10 11 12 13 14
Day 3   JHT JHT JHT   15 16 17 18 19 20 21
Day 4   JHT JHT   22 23 24 25 26 27 28 29
Day 5   JHT   30 31 32 33 34 35 36 37 38
           39 40 41 42 43 44 45

Once a week for seven weeks: 1 2 3 4 5 6 7
Once a month: Jan Feb Mar Apr May Jun Jul Aug Sep Oct Nov Dec

---

18. Proverbs 28:13

He that covereth his sins shall not prosper: but whoso confesseth and forsaketh them shall have mercy.

1st 5 days   **Next 45 days**

Day 1   JHT JHT JHT JHT JHT   1 2 3 4 5 6 7 8
Day 2   JHT JHT JHT JHT   9 10 11 12 13 14
Day 3   JHT JHT JHT   15 16 17 18 19 20 21
Day 4   JHT JHT   22 23 24 25 26 27 28 29
Day 5   JHT   30 31 32 33 34 35 36 37 38
           39 40 41 42 43 44 45

Once a week for seven weeks: 1 2 3 4 5 6 7
Once a month: Jan Feb Mar Apr May Jun Jul Aug Sep Oct Nov Dec

---

19. Memorize John 12:24

Verily, verily, I say unto you, Except a corn of wheat fall into the ground and die, it abideth alone: but if it die, it bringeth forth much fruit.

1st 5 days   **Next 45 days**

Day 1   JHT JHT JHT JHT JHT   1 2 3 4 5 6 7 8
Day 2   JHT JHT JHT JHT   9 10 11 12 13 14
Day 3   JHT JHT JHT   15 16 17 18 19 20 21
Day 4   JHT JHT   22 23 24 25 26 27 28 29
Day 5   JHT   30 31 32 33 34 35 36 37 38
           39 40 41 42 43 44 45

Once a week for seven weeks: 1 2 3 4 5 6 7
Once a month: Jan Feb Mar Apr May Jun Jul Aug Sep Oct Nov Dec

---

20. Luke 9:23-24

And he said to them all, If any man will come after me, let him deny himself, and take up his cross daily, and follow me. For whosoever will save his life shall lose it: but whosoever will lose his life for my sake, the same shall save it.

1st 5 days   **Next 45 days**

Day 1   JHT JHT JHT JHT JHT   1 2 3 4 5 6 7 8
Day 2   JHT JHT JHT JHT   9 10 11 12 13 14
Day 3   JHT JHT JHT   15 16 17 18 19 20 21
Day 4   JHT JHT   22 23 24 25 26 27 28 29
Day 5   JHT   30 31 32 33 34 35 36 37 38
           39 40 41 42 43 44 45

Once a week for seven weeks: 1 2 3 4 5 6 7
Once a month: Jan Feb Mar Apr May Jun Jul Aug Sep Oct Nov Dec

21. Romans 8:13

For if ye live after the flesh, ye shall die: but if ye through the Spirit do mortify the deeds of the body, ye shall live.

1st 5 days   **Next 45 days**

Day 1	~~卌 卌 卌 卌 卌~~	1 2 3 4 5 6 7 8
Day 2	~~卌 卌 卌 卌~~	9 10 11 12 13 14
Day 3	~~卌 卌 卌~~	15 16 17 18 19 20 21
Day 4	~~卌 卌~~	22 23 24 25 26 27 28 29
Day 5	~~卌~~	30 31 32 33 34 35 36 37 38
		39 40 41 42 43 44 45

Once a week for seven weeks: 1 2 3 4 5 6 7
Once a month: Jan Feb Mar Apr May Jun Jul Aug Sep Oct Nov Dec

---

22. Romans 6:6

Knowing this, that our old man is crucified with him, that the body of sin might be destroyed, that henceforth we should not serve sin.

1st 5 days   **Next 45 days**

Day 1	~~卌 卌 卌 卌 卌~~	1 2 3 4 5 6 7 8
Day 2	~~卌 卌 卌 卌~~	9 10 11 12 13 14
Day 3	~~卌 卌 卌~~	15 16 17 18 19 20 21
Day 4	~~卌 卌~~	22 23 24 25 26 27 28 29
Day 5	~~卌~~	30 31 32 33 34 35 36 37 38
		39 40 41 42 43 44 45

Once a week for seven weeks: 1 2 3 4 5 6 7
Once a month: Jan Feb Mar Apr May Jun Jul Aug Sep Oct Nov Dec

---

23. Romans 6:9-12

Knowing that Christ being raised from the dead dieth no more; death hath no more dominion over him. For in that he died, he died unto sin once: but in that he liveth, he liveth unto God. Likewise, reckon ye also yourselves to be dead indeed unto sin, but alive unto God through Jesus Christ our Lord. Let not sin therefore reign in your mortal body, that ye should obey it in the lusts thereof.

1st 5 days   **Next 45 days**

Day 1	~~卌 卌 卌 卌 卌~~	1 2 3 4 5 6 7 8
Day 2	~~卌 卌 卌 卌~~	9 10 11 12 13 14
Day 3	~~卌 卌 卌~~	15 16 17 18 19 20 21
Day 4	~~卌 卌~~	22 23 24 25 26 27 28 29
Day 5	~~卌~~	30 31 32 33 34 35 36 37 38
		39 40 41 42 43 44 45

Once a week for seven weeks: 1 2 3 4 5 6 7
Once a month: Jan Feb Mar Apr May Jun Jul Aug Sep Oct Nov Dec

---

24. Romans 6:13-14

Neither yield ye your members as instruments of unrighteousness unto sin: but yield yourselves unto God, as those that are alive from the dead, and your members as instruments of righteousness unto God. For sin shall not have dominion over you: for ye are not under the law, but under grace.

1st 5 days   **Next 45 days**

Day 1	~~卌 卌 卌 卌 卌~~	1 2 3 4 5 6 7 8
Day 2	~~卌 卌 卌 卌~~	9 10 11 12 13 14
Day 3	~~卌 卌 卌~~	15 16 17 18 19 20 21
Day 4	~~卌 卌~~	22 23 24 25 26 27 28 29
Day 5	~~卌~~	30 31 32 33 34 35 36 37 38
		39 40 41 42 43 44 45

Once a week for seven weeks: 1 2 3 4 5 6 7
Once a month: Jan Feb Mar Apr May Jun Jul Aug Sep Oct Nov Dec

1st 5 days   **Next 45 days**

25. Romans 8:12-13

Therefore, brethren, we are debtors, not to the flesh, to live after the flesh. For if ye live after the flesh, ye shall die: but if ye through the Spirit do mortify the deeds of the body, ye shall live.

Day 1   JHT JHT JHT JHT JHT   1 2 3 4 5 6 7 8
Day 2   JHT JHT JHT JHT   9 10 11 12 13 14
Day 3   JHT JHT JHT   15 16 17 18 19 20 21
Day 4   JHT JHT   22 23 24 25 26 27 28 29
Day 5   JHT   30 31 32 33 34 35 36 37 38
     39 40 41 42 43 44 45

Once a week for seven weeks: 1 2 3 4 5 6 7
Once a month: Jan Feb Mar Apr May Jun Jul Aug Sep Oct Nov Dec

---

WINNING LIFE'S BATTLES   THROUGH JESUS CHRIST

1st 5 days   **Next 45 days**

26. 1 Corinthians 15:57-58

But thanks be to God, which giveth us the victory through our Lord Jesus Christ. Therefore, my beloved brethren, be ye steadfast, unmoveable, always abounding in the work of the Lord, forasmuch as ye know that your labour is not in vain in the Lord.

Day 1   JHT JHT JHT JHT JHT   1 2 3 4 5 6 7 8
Day 2   JHT JHT JHT JHT   9 10 11 12 13 14
Day 3   JHT JHT JHT   15 16 17 18 19 20 21
Day 4   JHT JHT   22 23 24 25 26 27 28 29
Day 5   JHT   30 31 32 33 34 35 36 37 38
     39 40 41 42 43 44 45

Once a week for seven weeks: 1 2 3 4 5 6 7
Once a month: Jan Feb Mar Apr May Jun Jul Aug Sep Oct Nov Dec

---

WINNING LIFE'S BATTLES   THROUGH JESUS CHRIST

1st 5 days   **Next 45 days**

27. Romans 6:16-18

Know ye not, that to whom ye yield yourselves servants to obey, his servants ye are to whom ye obey; whether of sin unto death, or of obedience unto righteousness? But God be thanked, that ye were the servants of sin, but ye have obeyed from the heart that form of doctrine which was delivered you. Being then made free from sin, ye became the servants of righteousness.

Day 1   JHT JHT JHT JHT JHT   1 2 3 4 5 6 7 8
Day 2   JHT JHT JHT JHT   9 10 11 12 13 14
Day 3   JHT JHT JHT   15 16 17 18 19 20 21
Day 4   JHT JHT   22 23 24 25 26 27 28 29
Day 5   JHT   30 31 32 33 34 35 36 37 38
     39 40 41 42 43 44 45

Once a week for seven weeks: 1 2 3 4 5 6 7
Once a month: Jan Feb Mar Apr May Jun Jul Aug Sep Oct Nov Dec

---

WINNING LIFE'S BATTLES   THROUGH JESUS CHRIST

1st 5 days   **Next 45 days**

28. Romans 6:19

For as ye have yielded your members servants to uncleanness and to iniquity unto iniquity; even so now yield your members servants to righteousness unto holiness.

Day 1   JHT JHT JHT JHT JHT   1 2 3 4 5 6 7 8
Day 2   JHT JHT JHT JHT   9 10 11 12 13 14
Day 3   JHT JHT JHT   15 16 17 18 19 20 21
Day 4   JHT JHT   22 23 24 25 26 27 28 29
Day 5   JHT   30 31 32 33 34 35 36 37 38
     39 40 41 42 43 44 45

Once a week for seven weeks: 1 2 3 4 5 6 7
Once a month: Jan Feb Mar Apr May Jun Jul Aug Sep Oct Nov Dec

Card 29

29. Galatians 6:7-9

Be not deceived; God is not mocked: for whatsoever a man soweth, that shall he also reap. For he that soweth to his flesh shall of the flesh reap corruption; but he that soweth to the Spirit shall of the Spirit reap life everlasting. And let us not be weary in well doing: for in due season we shall reap, if we faint not.

1st 5 days   **Next 45 days**

Day 1 ∭ ∭ ∭ ∭ ∭   1 2 3 4 5 6 7 8
Day 2 ∭ ∭ ∭ ∭   9 10 11 12 13 14
Day 3 ∭ ∭ ∭   15 16 17 18 19 20 21
Day 4 ∭ ∭   22 23 24 25 26 27 28 29
Day 5 ∭   30 31 32 33 34 35 36 37 38
                          39 40 41 42 43 44 45

Once a week for seven weeks: 1 2 3 4 5 6 7
Once a month: Jan Feb Mar Apr May Jun Jul Aug Sep Oct Nov Dec

---

Card 30

30. Romans 13:14

But put ye on the Lord Jesus Christ, and make not provision for the flesh, to fulfill the lusts thereof.

1st 5 days   **Next 45 days**

Day 1 ∭ ∭ ∭ ∭ ∭   1 2 3 4 5 6 7 8
Day 2 ∭ ∭ ∭ ∭   9 10 11 12 13 14
Day 3 ∭ ∭ ∭   15 16 17 18 19 20 21
Day 4 ∭ ∭   22 23 24 25 26 27 28 29
Day 5 ∭   30 31 32 33 34 35 36 37 38
                          39 40 41 42 43 44 45

Once a week for seven weeks: 1 2 3 4 5 6 7
Once a month: Jan Feb Mar Apr May Jun Jul Aug Sep Oct Nov Dec

---

Card 31

31. Psalm 139:23-24

Search me, O God, and know my heart: try me, and know my thoughts: And see if there be any wicked way in me, and lead me in the way everlasting.

1st 5 days   **Next 45 days**

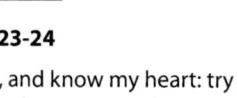

Day 1 ∭ ∭ ∭ ∭ ∭   1 2 3 4 5 6 7 8
Day 2 ∭ ∭ ∭ ∭   9 10 11 12 13 14
Day 3 ∭ ∭ ∭   15 16 17 18 19 20 21
Day 4 ∭ ∭   22 23 24 25 26 27 28 29
Day 5 ∭   30 31 32 33 34 35 36 37 38
                          39 40 41 42 43 44 45

Once a week for seven weeks: 1 2 3 4 5 6 7
Once a month: Jan Feb Mar Apr May Jun Jul Aug Sep Oct Nov Dec

---

Card 32

32. Jeremiah 2:13

For my people have committed two evils; they have forsaken me the fountain of living waters, and hewed them out cisterns, broken cisterns that can hold no water.

1st 5 days   **Next 45 days**

Day 1 ∭ ∭ ∭ ∭ ∭   1 2 3 4 5 6 7 8
Day 2 ∭ ∭ ∭ ∭   9 10 11 12 13 14
Day 3 ∭ ∭ ∭   15 16 17 18 19 20 21
Day 4 ∭ ∭   22 23 24 25 26 27 28 29
Day 5 ∭   30 31 32 33 34 35 36 37 38
                          39 40 41 42 43 44 45

Once a week for seven weeks: 1 2 3 4 5 6 7
Once a month: Jan Feb Mar Apr May Jun Jul Aug Sep Oct Nov Dec

33. John 15:4-5

Abide in me, and I in you. As the branch cannot bear fruit of itself, except it abide in the vine; no more can ye, except ye abide in me. I am the vine, ye are the branches: He that abideth in me, and I in him, the same bringeth forth much fruit: for without me ye can do nothing.

1st 5 days   **Next 45 days**

Day 1	~~JHT JHT JHT JHT JHT~~	1 2 3 4 5 6 7 8
Day 2	~~JHT JHT JHT JHT~~	9 10 11 12 13 14
Day 3	~~JHT JHT JHT~~	15 16 17 18 19 20 21
Day 4	~~JHT JHT~~	22 23 24 25 26 27 28 29
Day 5	~~JHT~~	30 31 32 33 34 35 36 37 38
		39 40 41 42 43 44 45

Once a week for seven weeks: 1 2 3 4 5 6 7
Once a month: Jan Feb Mar Apr May Jun Jul Aug Sep Oct Nov Dec

---

34. Psalm 42:1-2

As the hart panteth after the water brooks, so panteth my soul after thee, O God. My soul thirsteth for God, for the living God.

1st 5 days   **Next 45 days**

Day 1	~~JHT JHT JHT JHT JHT~~	1 2 3 4 5 6 7 8
Day 2	~~JHT JHT JHT JHT~~	9 10 11 12 13 14
Day 3	~~JHT JHT JHT~~	15 16 17 18 19 20 21
Day 4	~~JHT JHT~~	22 23 24 25 26 27 28 29
Day 5	~~JHT~~	30 31 32 33 34 35 36 37 38
		39 40 41 42 43 44 45

Once a week for seven weeks: 1 2 3 4 5 6 7
Once a month: Jan Feb Mar Apr May Jun Jul Aug Sep Oct Nov Dec

---

35. 1 John 4:9-10

In this was manifest the love of God toward us, because that God sent his only begotten Son into the world, that we might live through him. Herein is love, not that we loved God, but that he loved us, and sent his Son to be the propitiation for our sins.

1st 5 days   **Next 45 days**

Day 1	~~JHT JHT JHT JHT JHT~~	1 2 3 4 5 6 7 8
Day 2	~~JHT JHT JHT JHT~~	9 10 11 12 13 14
Day 3	~~JHT JHT JHT~~	15 16 17 18 19 20 21
Day 4	~~JHT JHT~~	22 23 24 25 26 27 28 29
Day 5	~~JHT~~	30 31 32 33 34 35 36 37 38
		39 40 41 42 43 44 45

Once a week for seven weeks: 1 2 3 4 5 6 7
Once a month: Jan Feb Mar Apr May Jun Jul Aug Sep Oct Nov Dec

---

36. 1 John 3:1-3

Behold, what manner of love the Father hath bestowed upon us, that we should be called the sons of God: therefore the world knoweth us not, because it knew him not. Beloved, now are we the sons of God, and it doth not yet appear what we shall be: but we know that when he shall appear, we shall be like him; for we shall see him as he is. And everyone that hath this hope in him purifieth himself, even as he is pure.

1st 5 days   **Next 45 days**

Day 1	~~JHT JHT JHT JHT JHT~~	1 2 3 4 5 6 7 8
Day 2	~~JHT JHT JHT JHT~~	9 10 11 12 13 14
Day 3	~~JHT JHT JHT~~	15 16 17 18 19 20 21
Day 4	~~JHT JHT~~	22 23 24 25 26 27 28 29
Day 5	~~JHT~~	30 31 32 33 34 35 36 37 38
		39 40 41 42 43 44 45

Once a week for seven weeks: 1 2 3 4 5 6 7
Once a month: Jan Feb Mar Apr May Jun Jul Aug Sep Oct Nov Dec

37. Jeremiah 31:3

The Lord hath appeared of old unto me, saying, Yea, I have loved thee with an everlasting love: therefore with lovingkindness have I drawn thee.

1st 5 days   **Next 45 days**

Day 1   ~~LHT LHT LHT LHT LHT~~   1 2 3 4 5 6 7 8
Day 2   ~~LHT LHT LHT LHT~~   9 10 11 12 13 14
Day 3   ~~LHT LHT LHT~~   15 16 17 18 19 20 21
Day 4   ~~LHT LHT~~   22 23 24 25 26 27 28 29
Day 5   ~~LHT~~   30 31 32 33 34 35 36 37 38
     39 40 41 42 43 44 45

Once a week for seven weeks: 1 2 3 4 5 6 7
Once a month: Jan Feb Mar Apr May Jun Jul Aug Sep Oct Nov Dec

---

 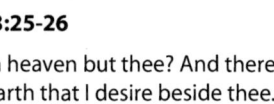

38. Psalm 63:1

O God, thou art my God; early will I seek thee: my soul thirsteth for thee, my flesh longeth for thee in a dry and thirsty land, where no water is.

1st 5 days   **Next 45 days**

Day 1   ~~LHT LHT LHT LHT LHT~~   1 2 3 4 5 6 7 8
Day 2   ~~LHT LHT LHT LHT~~   9 10 11 12 13 14
Day 3   ~~LHT LHT LHT~~   15 16 17 18 19 20 21
Day 4   ~~LHT LHT~~   22 23 24 25 26 27 28 29
Day 5   ~~LHT~~   30 31 32 33 34 35 36 37 38
     39 40 41 42 43 44 45

Once a week for seven weeks: 1 2 3 4 5 6 7
Once a month: Jan Feb Mar Apr May Jun Jul Aug Sep Oct Nov Dec

---

39. Psalm 73:25-26

Whom have I in heaven but thee? And there is none upon earth that I desire beside thee. My flesh and my heart faileth: but God is the strength of my heart, and my portion for ever.

1st 5 days   **Next 45 days**

Day 1   ~~LHT LHT LHT LHT LHT~~   1 2 3 4 5 6 7 8
Day 2   ~~LHT LHT LHT LHT~~   9 10 11 12 13 14
Day 3   ~~LHT LHT LHT~~   15 16 17 18 19 20 21
Day 4   ~~LHT LHT~~   22 23 24 25 26 27 28 29
Day 5   ~~LHT~~   30 31 32 33 34 35 36 37 38
     39 40 41 42 43 44 45

Once a week for seven weeks: 1 2 3 4 5 6 7
Once a month: Jan Feb Mar Apr May Jun Jul Aug Sep Oct Nov Dec

---

40. Psalm 84:2

My soul longeth, yea, even fainteth for the courts of the Lord: my heart and my flesh crieth out for the living God.

1st 5 days   **Next 45 days**

Day 1   ~~LHT LHT LHT LHT LHT~~   1 2 3 4 5 6 7 8
Day 2   ~~LHT LHT LHT LHT~~   9 10 11 12 13 14
Day 3   ~~LHT LHT LHT~~   15 16 17 18 19 20 21
Day 4   ~~LHT LHT~~   22 23 24 25 26 27 28 29
Day 5   ~~LHT~~   30 31 32 33 34 35 36 37 38
     39 40 41 42 43 44 45

Once a week for seven weeks: 1 2 3 4 5 6 7
Once a month: Jan Feb Mar Apr May Jun Jul Aug Sep Oct Nov Dec

41. Deuteronomy 4:29

But if from thence thou shalt seek the Lord thy God, thou shalt find him, if thou seek him with all thy heart and with all thy soul.

1st 5 days   **Next 45 days**

Day 1   ⊬⊬⊬ ⊬⊬⊬ ⊬⊬⊬ ⊬⊬⊬ ⊬⊬⊬   1 2 3 4 5 6 7 8
Day 2   ⊬⊬⊬ ⊬⊬⊬ ⊬⊬⊬ ⊬⊬⊬   9 10 11 12 13 14
Day 3   ⊬⊬⊬ ⊬⊬⊬ ⊬⊬⊬   15 16 17 18 19 20 21
Day 4   ⊬⊬⊬ ⊬⊬⊬   22 23 24 25 26 27 28 29
Day 5   ⊬⊬⊬   30 31 32 33 34 35 36 37 38
     39 40 41 42 43 44 45

Once a week for seven weeks: 1 2 3 4 5 6 7
Once a month: Jan Feb Mar Apr May Jun Jul Aug Sep Oct Nov Dec

---

42. Matthew 6:24

No man can serve two masters: for either he will hate the one, and love the other; or else he will hold to the one, and despise the other. Ye cannot serve God and mammon.

1st 5 days   **Next 45 days**

Day 1   ⊬⊬⊬ ⊬⊬⊬ ⊬⊬⊬ ⊬⊬⊬ ⊬⊬⊬   1 2 3 4 5 6 7 8
Day 2   ⊬⊬⊬ ⊬⊬⊬ ⊬⊬⊬ ⊬⊬⊬   9 10 11 12 13 14
Day 3   ⊬⊬⊬ ⊬⊬⊬ ⊬⊬⊬   15 16 17 18 19 20 21
Day 4   ⊬⊬⊬ ⊬⊬⊬   22 23 24 25 26 27 28 29
Day 5   ⊬⊬⊬   30 31 32 33 34 35 36 37 38
     39 40 41 42 43 44 45

Once a week for seven weeks: 1 2 3 4 5 6 7
Once a month: Jan Feb Mar Apr May Jun Jul Aug Sep Oct Nov Dec

---

43. James 4:4, 8, 10

Ye adulterers and adulteresses, know ye not that the friendship of the world is enmity with God? Whosoever therefore will be a friend of the world is the enemy of God. . . Draw nigh to God, and he will draw nigh to you. Cleanse your hands, ye sinners; and purify your hearts, ye double minded. . . Humble yourselves in the sight of the Lord, and he shall lift you up.

1st 5 days   **Next 45 days**

Day 1   ⊬⊬⊬ ⊬⊬⊬ ⊬⊬⊬ ⊬⊬⊬ ⊬⊬⊬   1 2 3 4 5 6 7 8
Day 2   ⊬⊬⊬ ⊬⊬⊬ ⊬⊬⊬ ⊬⊬⊬   9 10 11 12 13 14
Day 3   ⊬⊬⊬ ⊬⊬⊬ ⊬⊬⊬   15 16 17 18 19 20 21
Day 4   ⊬⊬⊬ ⊬⊬⊬   22 23 24 25 26 27 28 29
Day 5   ⊬⊬⊬   30 31 32 33 34 35 36 37 38
     39 40 41 42 43 44 45

Once a week for seven weeks: 1 2 3 4 5 6 7
Once a month: Jan Feb Mar Apr May Jun Jul Aug Sep Oct Nov Dec

---

44. Psalm 1:1-2

Blessed is the man that walketh not in the counsel of the ungodly, nor standeth in the way of sinners, nor sitteth in the seat of the scornful. But his delight is in the law of the Lord: and in his law doth he meditate both day and night.

1st 5 days   **Next 45 days**

Day 1   ⊬⊬⊬ ⊬⊬⊬ ⊬⊬⊬ ⊬⊬⊬ ⊬⊬⊬   1 2 3 4 5 6 7 8
Day 2   ⊬⊬⊬ ⊬⊬⊬ ⊬⊬⊬ ⊬⊬⊬   9 10 11 12 13 14
Day 3   ⊬⊬⊬ ⊬⊬⊬ ⊬⊬⊬   15 16 17 18 19 20 21
Day 4   ⊬⊬⊬ ⊬⊬⊬   22 23 24 25 26 27 28 29
Day 5   ⊬⊬⊬   30 31 32 33 34 35 36 37 38
     39 40 41 42 43 44 45

Once a week for seven weeks: 1 2 3 4 5 6 7
Once a month: Jan Feb Mar Apr May Jun Jul Aug Sep Oct Nov Dec

WINNING LIFE'S BATTLES — THROUGH JESUS CHRIST

45. Psalm 1:3

And he shall be like a tree planted by the rivers of water, that bringeth forth his fruit in his season: his leaf also shall not wither; and whatsoever he doeth shall prosper.

1st 5 days	Next 45 days
Day 1 LHT LHT LHT LHT LHT	1 2 3 4 5 6 7 8
Day 2 LHT LHT LHT LHT	9 10 11 12 13 14
Day 3 LHT LHT LHT	15 16 17 18 19 20 21
Day 4 LHT LHT	22 23 24 25 26 27 28 29
Day 5 LHT	30 31 32 33 34 35 36 37 38
	39 40 41 42 43 44 45

Once a week for seven weeks: 1 2 3 4 5 6 7
Once a month: Jan Feb Mar Apr May Jun Jul Aug Sep Oct Nov Dec

---

WINNING LIFE'S BATTLES — THROUGH JESUS CHRIST

46. Psalm 1:4-5

The ungodly are not so: but are like the chaff which the wind driveth away. Therefore the ungodly shall not stand in the judgment, nor sinners in the congregation of the righteous.

1st 5 days	Next 45 days
Day 1 LHT LHT LHT LHT LHT	1 2 3 4 5 6 7 8
Day 2 LHT LHT LHT LHT	9 10 11 12 13 14
Day 3 LHT LHT LHT	15 16 17 18 19 20 21
Day 4 LHT LHT	22 23 24 25 26 27 28 29
Day 5 LHT	30 31 32 33 34 35 36 37 38
	39 40 41 42 43 44 45

Once a week for seven weeks: 1 2 3 4 5 6 7
Once a month: Jan Feb Mar Apr May Jun Jul Aug Sep Oct Nov Dec

---

WINNING LIFE'S BATTLES — THROUGH JESUS CHRIST

47. 2 Corinthians 3:18

But we all, with open face beholding as in a glass the glory of the Lord, are changed into the same image from glory to glory, even as by the Spirit of the Lord.

1st 5 days	Next 45 days
Day 1 LHT LHT LHT LHT LHT	1 2 3 4 5 6 7 8
Day 2 LHT LHT LHT LHT	9 10 11 12 13 14
Day 3 LHT LHT LHT	15 16 17 18 19 20 21
Day 4 LHT LHT	22 23 24 25 26 27 28 29
Day 5 LHT	30 31 32 33 34 35 36 37 38
	39 40 41 42 43 44 45

Once a week for seven weeks: 1 2 3 4 5 6 7
Once a month: Jan Feb Mar Apr May Jun Jul Aug Sep Oct Nov Dec

---

WINNING LIFE'S BATTLES — THROUGH JESUS CHRIST

48. Memorize John 1:14

And the Word was made flesh, and dwelt among us, (and we beheld his glory, the glory as of the only begotten of the Father,) full of grace and truth.

1st 5 days	Next 45 days
Day 1 LHT LHT LHT LHT LHT	1 2 3 4 5 6 7 8
Day 2 LHT LHT LHT LHT	9 10 11 12 13 14
Day 3 LHT LHT LHT	15 16 17 18 19 20 21
Day 4 LHT LHT	22 23 24 25 26 27 28 29
Day 5 LHT	30 31 32 33 34 35 36 37 38
	39 40 41 42 43 44 45

Once a week for seven weeks: 1 2 3 4 5 6 7
Once a month: Jan Feb Mar Apr May Jun Jul Aug Sep Oct Nov Dec

49. James 1:22-23

But be ye doers of the word, and not hearers only, deceiving your own selves. For if any be a hearer of the word, and not a doer, he is like unto a man beholding his natural face in a glass:

1st 5 days   **Next 45 days**

Day 1   J̶H̶T̶ J̶H̶T̶ J̶H̶T̶ J̶H̶T̶ J̶H̶T̶   1 2 3 4 5 6 7 8
Day 2   J̶H̶T̶ J̶H̶T̶ J̶H̶T̶ J̶H̶T̶   9 10 11 12 13 14
Day 3   J̶H̶T̶ J̶H̶T̶ J̶H̶T̶   15 16 17 18 19 20 21
Day 4   J̶H̶T̶ J̶H̶T̶   22 23 24 25 26 27 28 29
Day 5   J̶H̶T̶   30 31 32 33 34 35 36 37 38
        39 40 41 42 43 44 45

Once a week for seven weeks: 1 2 3 4 5 6 7
Once a month: Jan Feb Mar Apr May Jun Jul Aug Sep Oct Nov Dec

---

50. James 1:24-25

For he beholdeth himself, and goeth his way, and straightway forgetteth what manner of man he was. But whoso looketh into the perfect law of liberty, and continueth therein, he being not a forgetful hearer, but a doer of the work, this man shall be blessed in his deed.

1st 5 days   **Next 45 days**

Day 1   J̶H̶T̶ J̶H̶T̶ J̶H̶T̶ J̶H̶T̶ J̶H̶T̶   1 2 3 4 5 6 7 8
Day 2   J̶H̶T̶ J̶H̶T̶ J̶H̶T̶ J̶H̶T̶   9 10 11 12 13 14
Day 3   J̶H̶T̶ J̶H̶T̶ J̶H̶T̶   15 16 17 18 19 20 21
Day 4   J̶H̶T̶ J̶H̶T̶   22 23 24 25 26 27 28 29
Day 5   J̶H̶T̶   30 31 32 33 34 35 36 37 38
        39 40 41 42 43 44 45

Once a week for seven weeks: 1 2 3 4 5 6 7
Once a month: Jan Feb Mar Apr May Jun Jul Aug Sep Oct Nov Dec

---

51. Philippians 2:3-4

Let nothing be done through strife or vainglory; but in lowliness of mind let each esteem other better than themselves. Look not every man on his own things, but every man also on the things of others.

1st 5 days   **Next 45 days**

Day 1   J̶H̶T̶ J̶H̶T̶ J̶H̶T̶ J̶H̶T̶ J̶H̶T̶   1 2 3 4 5 6 7 8
Day 2   J̶H̶T̶ J̶H̶T̶ J̶H̶T̶ J̶H̶T̶   9 10 11 12 13 14
Day 3   J̶H̶T̶ J̶H̶T̶ J̶H̶T̶   15 16 17 18 19 20 21
Day 4   J̶H̶T̶ J̶H̶T̶   22 23 24 25 26 27 28 29
Day 5   J̶H̶T̶   30 31 32 33 34 35 36 37 38
        39 40 41 42 43 44 45

Once a week for seven weeks: 1 2 3 4 5 6 7
Once a month: Jan Feb Mar Apr May Jun Jul Aug Sep Oct Nov Dec

---

52. Philippians 5-7

Let this mind be in you, which was also in Christ Jesus: Who, being in the form of God, thought it not robbery to be equal with God: But made himself of no reputation, and took upon him the form of a servant, and was made in the likeness of men:

1st 5 days   **Next 45 days**

Day 1   J̶H̶T̶ J̶H̶T̶ J̶H̶T̶ J̶H̶T̶ J̶H̶T̶   1 2 3 4 5 6 7 8
Day 2   J̶H̶T̶ J̶H̶T̶ J̶H̶T̶ J̶H̶T̶   9 10 11 12 13 14
Day 3   J̶H̶T̶ J̶H̶T̶ J̶H̶T̶   15 16 17 18 19 20 21
Day 4   J̶H̶T̶ J̶H̶T̶   22 23 24 25 26 27 28 29
Day 5   J̶H̶T̶   30 31 32 33 34 35 36 37 38
        39 40 41 42 43 44 45

Once a week for seven weeks: 1 2 3 4 5 6 7
Once a month: Jan Feb Mar Apr May Jun Jul Aug Sep Oct Nov Dec

53. Philippians 2:8-10

And being found in fashion as a man, he humbled himself, and became obedient unto death, even the death of the cross. Wherefore God also hath highly exalted him, and given him a name which is above every name: That at the name of Jesus every knee should bow, of things in heaven, and things in earth, and things under the earth;

1st 5 days   **Next 45 days**

Day 1   JHT JHT JHT JHT JHT   1 2 3 4 5 6 7 8
Day 2   JHT JHT JHT JHT   9 10 11 12 13 14
Day 3   JHT JHT JHT   15 16 17 18 19 20 21
Day 4   JHT JHT   22 23 24 25 26 27 28 29
Day 5   JHT   30 31 32 33 34 35 36 37 38
                 39 40 41 42 43 44 45

Once a week for seven weeks: 1 2 3 4 5 6 7
Once a month: Jan Feb Mar Apr May Jun Jul Aug Sep Oct Nov Dec

---

54. Philippians 2:11-12

And that every tongue should confess that Jesus Christ is Lord, to the glory of God the Father. Wherefore, my beloved, as ye have always obeyed, not as in my presence only, but now much more in my absence, work out your own salvation with fear and trembling.

1st 5 days   **Next 45 days**

Day 1   JHT JHT JHT JHT JHT   1 2 3 4 5 6 7 8
Day 2   JHT JHT JHT JHT   9 10 11 12 13 14
Day 3   JHT JHT JHT   15 16 17 18 19 20 21
Day 4   JHT JHT   22 23 24 25 26 27 28 29
Day 5   JHT   30 31 32 33 34 35 36 37 38
                 39 40 41 42 43 44 45

Once a week for seven weeks: 1 2 3 4 5 6 7
Once a month: Jan Feb Mar Apr May Jun Jul Aug Sep Oct Nov Dec

---

55. Philippians 2:13-14

For it is God which worketh in you both to will and to do of his good pleasure. Do all things without murmurings and disputings:

1st 5 days   **Next 45 days**

Day 1   JHT JHT JHT JHT JHT   1 2 3 4 5 6 7 8
Day 2   JHT JHT JHT JHT   9 10 11 12 13 14
Day 3   JHT JHT JHT   15 16 17 18 19 20 21
Day 4   JHT JHT   22 23 24 25 26 27 28 29
Day 5   JHT   30 31 32 33 34 35 36 37 38
                 39 40 41 42 43 44 45

Once a week for seven weeks: 1 2 3 4 5 6 7
Once a month: Jan Feb Mar Apr May Jun Jul Aug Sep Oct Nov Dec

---

56. Philippians 2:15-16

That ye may be blameless and harmless, the sons of God, without rebuke, in the midst of a crooked and perverse nation, among whom ye shine as lights in the world; Holding forth the word of life; that I may rejoice in the day of Christ, that I have not run in vain, neither laboured in vain.

1st 5 days   **Next 45 days**

Day 1   JHT JHT JHT JHT JHT   1 2 3 4 5 6 7 8
Day 2   JHT JHT JHT JHT   9 10 11 12 13 14
Day 3   JHT JHT JHT   15 16 17 18 19 20 21
Day 4   JHT JHT   22 23 24 25 26 27 28 29
Day 5   JHT   30 31 32 33 34 35 36 37 38
                 39 40 41 42 43 44 45

Once a week for seven weeks: 1 2 3 4 5 6 7
Once a month: Jan Feb Mar Apr May Jun Jul Aug Sep Oct Nov Dec